REVISE 11+

Also available to support
Non-Verbal Reasoning 11+ revision:

Non-Verbal Reasoning

Practice Book 1

Series Consultant: Harry Smith
Author: Gareth Moore

THE REVISE 11+ SERIES

For the full range of Pearson Revise 11+ titles visit:
www.pearsonschools.co.uk/revise11plus

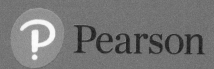

Contents

✓ How to use this book   1

✓ Diagnostic test   2

Transformations

✓ 1 Reflection   8

✓ 2 Rotation   12

Similarities and differences

✓ 3 Hidden shapes   16

✓ 4 Odd one out   20

✓ 5 Which image belongs?   24

✓ Checkpoint 1   28

Linear sequences

✓ 6 Complete the pair   30

✓ 7 Complete the series   34

Codes

✓ 8 Codes in boxes   38

✓ 9 Codes in lists   42

✓ Checkpoint 2   46

Nets

✓ 10 Parts of nets   48

✓ 11 Which cube does the net make?   52

✓ Checkpoint 3   56

Picturing things in 3D

✓ 12 Cube views   58

✓ 13 2D views of 3D solids   62

✓ 14 Fold along the line   66

✓ Progress test   70

✓ Answers   76

✓ Puzzle maker   96

✓ Cube nets   97

✓ Notes pages   98

✓ Progress chart   101

How to use this book

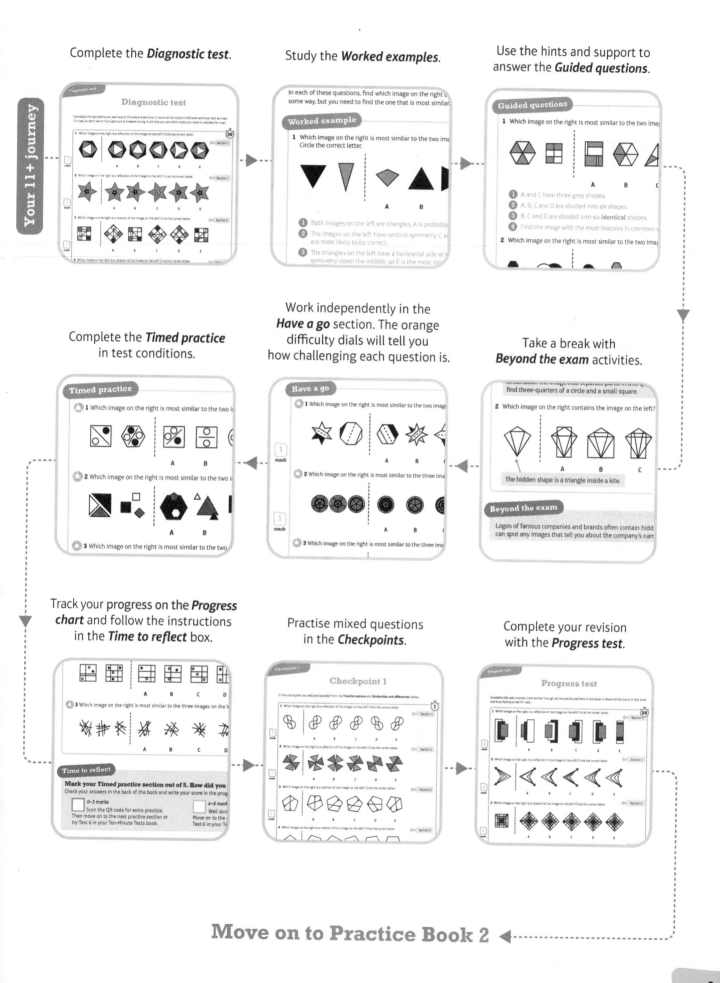

Complete the **Diagnostic test**.

Study the **Worked examples**.

Use the hints and support to answer the **Guided questions**.

Work independently in the **Have a go** section. The orange difficulty dials will tell you how challenging each question is.

Complete the **Timed practice** in test conditions.

Take a break with **Beyond the exam** activities.

Track your progress on the **Progress chart** and follow the instructions in the **Time to reflect** box.

Practise mixed questions in the **Checkpoints**.

Complete your revision with the **Progress test**.

Move on to Practice Book 2

Diagnostic test

Complete this test before you start any of the practice sections. It covers all the topics in this book and is as hard as a real 11+ test, so don't worry if you get a lot of answers wrong. It will help you see which topics you need to practise the most.

20

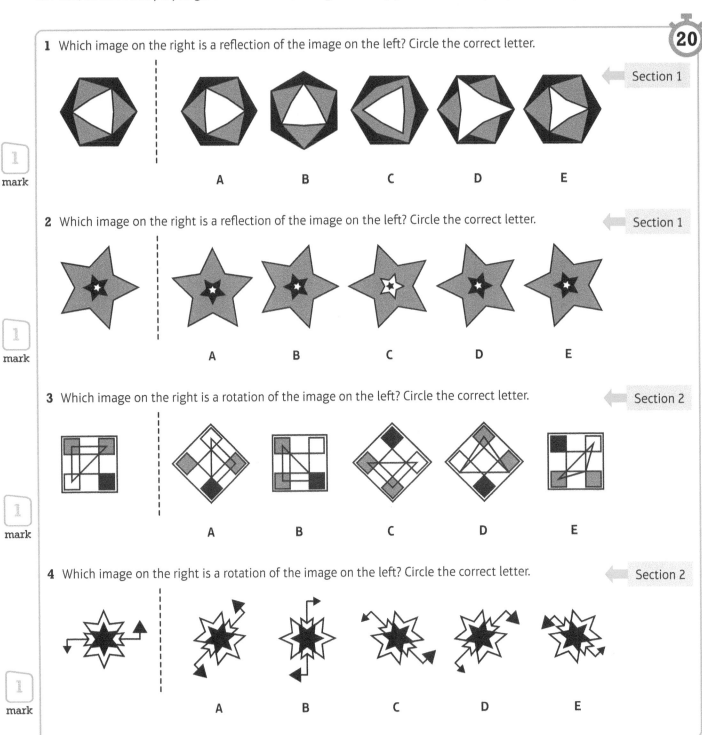

1 Which image on the right is a reflection of the image on the left? Circle the correct letter. ← Section 1

A   B   C   D   E

1 mark

2 Which image on the right is a reflection of the image on the left? Circle the correct letter. ← Section 1

A   B   C   D   E

1 mark

3 Which image on the right is a rotation of the image on the left? Circle the correct letter. ← Section 2

A   B   C   D   E

1 mark

4 Which image on the right is a rotation of the image on the left? Circle the correct letter. ← Section 2

A   B   C   D   E

1 mark

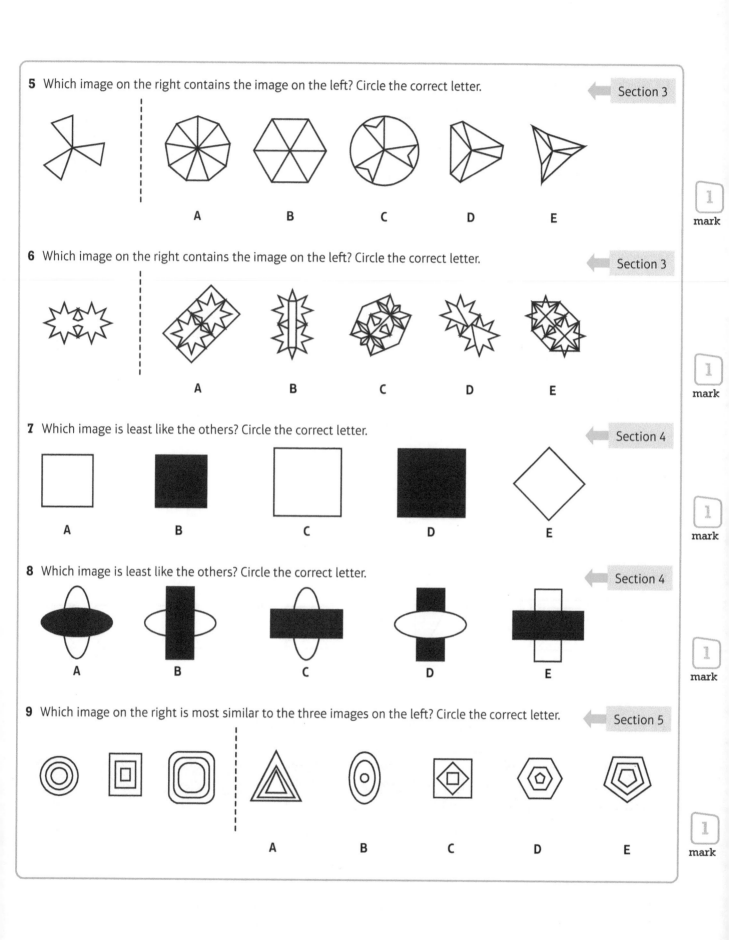

5 Which image on the right contains the image on the left? Circle the correct letter.

Section 3

A   B   C   D   E

1 mark

6 Which image on the right contains the image on the left? Circle the correct letter.

Section 3

A   B   C   D   E

1 mark

7 Which image is least like the others? Circle the correct letter.

Section 4

A   B   C   D   E

1 mark

8 Which image is least like the others? Circle the correct letter.

Section 4

A   B   C   D   E

1 mark

9 Which image on the right is most similar to the three images on the left? Circle the correct letter.

Section 5

A   B   C   D   E

1 mark

10 Which image on the right is most similar to the three images on the left? Circle the correct letter.   Section 5

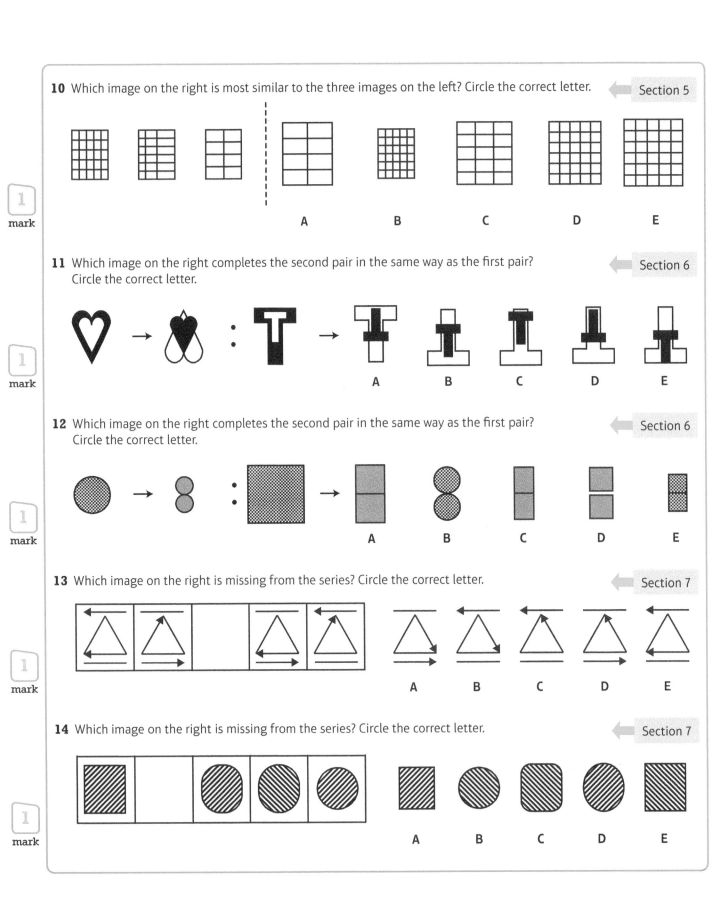

A   B   C   D   E

1 mark

11 Which image on the right completes the second pair in the same way as the first pair? Circle the correct letter.   Section 6

A   B   C   D   E

1 mark

12 Which image on the right completes the second pair in the same way as the first pair? Circle the correct letter.   Section 6

A   B   C   D   E

1 mark

13 Which image on the right is missing from the series? Circle the correct letter.   Section 7

A   B   C   D   E

1 mark

14 Which image on the right is missing from the series? Circle the correct letter.   Section 7

A   B   C   D   E

1 mark

15 Which code matches the final image? Circle the correct letter.

Section 8

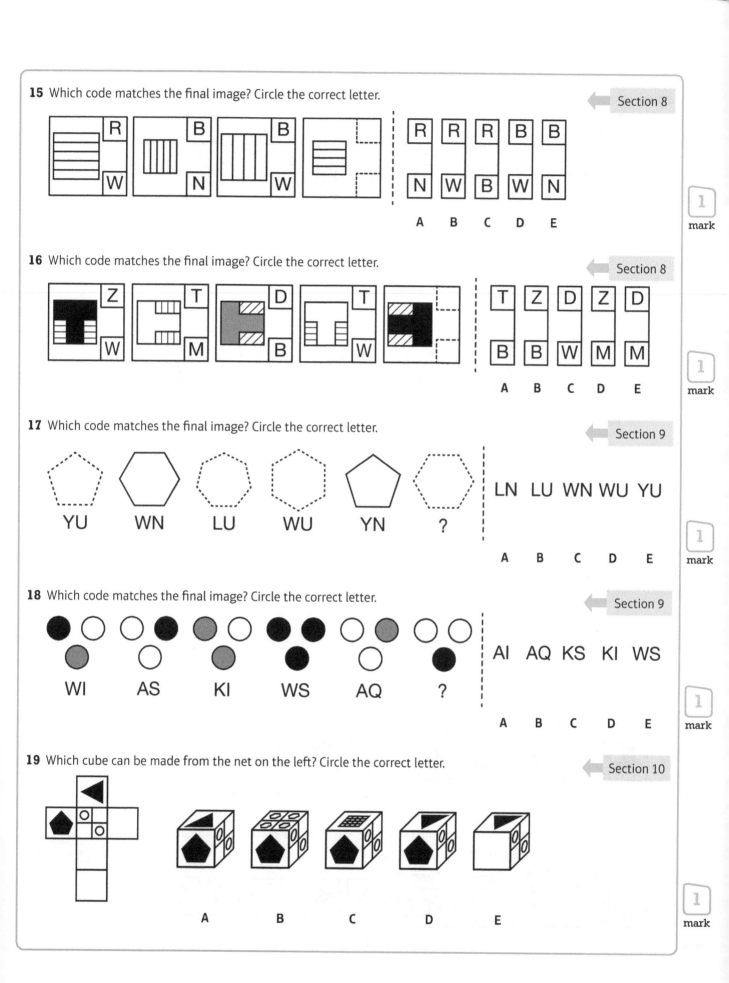

A B C D E

1 mark

16 Which code matches the final image? Circle the correct letter.

Section 8

A B C D E

1 mark

17 Which code matches the final image? Circle the correct letter.

Section 9

YU   WN   LU   WU   YN   ?

LN LU WN WU YU

A   B   C   D   E

1 mark

18 Which code matches the final image? Circle the correct letter.

Section 9

WI   AS   KI   WS   AQ   ?

AI AQ KS KI WS

A   B   C   D   E

1 mark

19 Which cube can be made from the net on the left? Circle the correct letter.

Section 10

A   B   C   D   E

1 mark

20 Which cube can be made from the net on the left? Circle the correct letter.

Section 10

A   B   C   D   E

1 mark

21 Which cube can be made from the net on the left? Circle the correct letter.

Section 11

A   B   C   D   E

1 mark

22 Which cube can be made from the net on the left? Circle the correct letter.

Section 11

A   B   C   D   E

1 mark

23 The first four images show rotations of the same cube. Which image on the right should replace the blank cube face? Circle the correct letter.

Section 12

A   B   C   D   E

1 mark

24 The first four images show rotations of the same cube. Which image on the right should replace the blank cube face? Circle the correct letter.

Section 12

A   B   C   D   E

1 mark

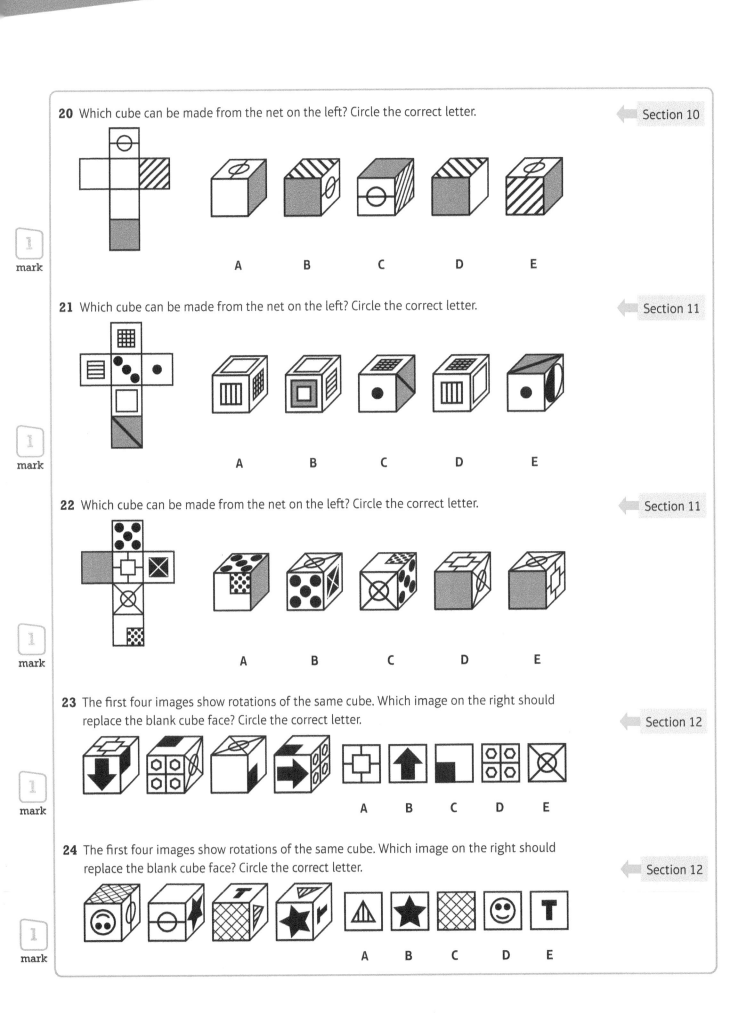

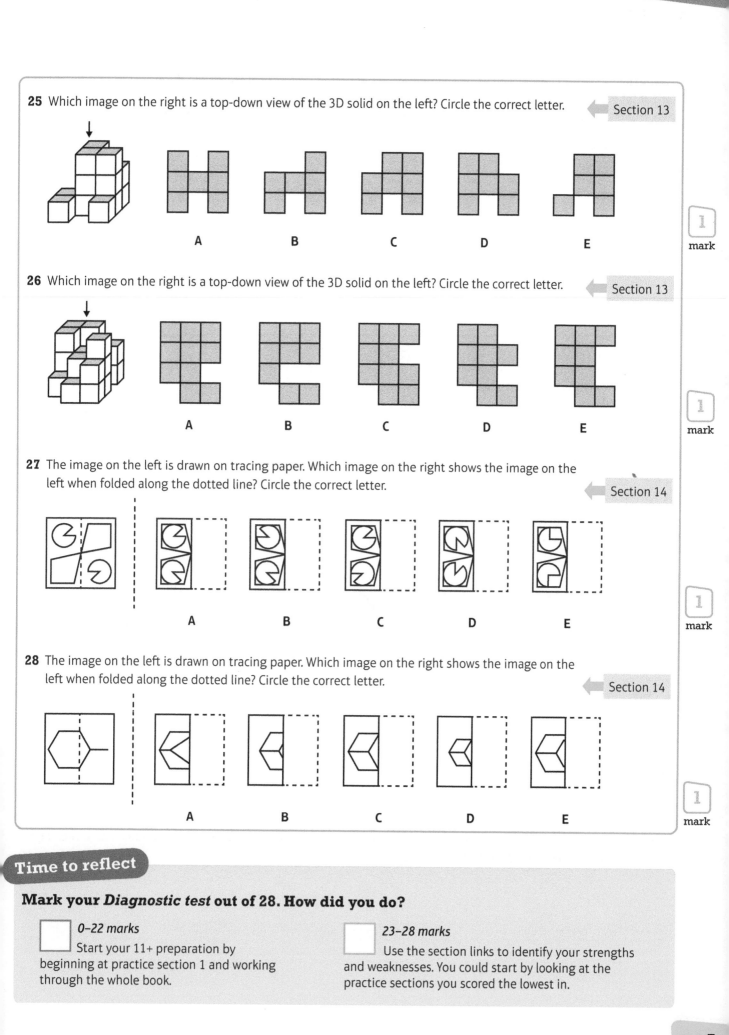

25 Which image on the right is a top-down view of the 3D solid on the left? Circle the correct letter. ← Section 13

A   B   C   D   E

1 mark

26 Which image on the right is a top-down view of the 3D solid on the left? Circle the correct letter. ← Section 13

A   B   C   D   E

1 mark

27 The image on the left is drawn on tracing paper. Which image on the right shows the image on the left when folded along the dotted line? Circle the correct letter. ← Section 14

A   B   C   D   E

1 mark

28 The image on the left is drawn on tracing paper. Which image on the right shows the image on the left when folded along the dotted line? Circle the correct letter. ← Section 14

A   B   C   D   E

1 mark

Time to reflect

Mark your *Diagnostic test* out of 28. How did you do?

☐ *0–22 marks*
Start your 11+ preparation by beginning at practice section 1 and working through the whole book.

☐ *23–28 marks*
Use the section links to identify your strengths and weaknesses. You could start by looking at the practice sections you scored the lowest in.

1 Reflection

A **reflection** is a mirror image of a shape. An image can be reflected in a **vertical** mirror line (flipped side-to-side) or in a **horizontal** mirror line (flipped upside down).
In each of these questions, find which of the five images on the right is the reflection of the image on the left.

Worked example

1 Which image on the right is a reflection of the image on the left? Circle the correct letter.

A   B   C   D   E

123 Imagine placing a mirror along the dashed line to reflect the image on the left. Choose the image after the dashed line that matches exactly the reflection you would see.

Look at the lines in the first image. There is a short diagonal line on the left and a long vertical line on the right.

Look at C. The short diagonal line is on the right. The long vertical line is on the left. This is the correct reflection of the first image.

Guided question

1 Which image on the right is a reflection of the image on the left? Circle the correct letter.

This image has two parts: the shape of a number 3 and the shape of a number 4. Look at the parts separately.

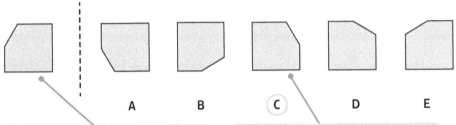

A   B   C   D   E

1 In the first image, the 3 is on the left, so the correct answer must have the 3 on the right. This means A and C must be wrong. Cross them out.

2 In the first image, the 3 is the right way around and the 4 is the wrong way around. Use this to help you work out whether the correct answer is B or D.

Beyond the exam

Draw a simple image and then draw a reflection of it. Use a real mirror to see how accurate your reflection is. This will be easier on graph paper, if you have some.

Guided questions

1 Which image on the right is a reflection of the image on the left? Circle the correct letter.

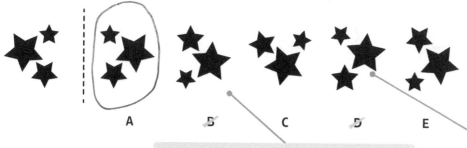

A   B   C   D   E

123 When a picture is reflected in a **vertical** mirror line, the parts of the image don't rotate or move up or down.

In the image on the left, the smallest star is at the top. In B it is at the bottom, so B cannot be a reflection of the first image.

In D, one point on the medium star is sticking straight up. In the image on the left, none of the points are sticking straight up, so the star in D has been rotated, not reflected.

2 Which image on the right is a reflection of the image on the left? Circle the correct letter.

A   B   C   D   E

The image on the left has two black circles with parts cut out of each. Look for the image on the right that shows the reflection of these cut-outs.

D looks very different and has different colours. You can cross it out straight away.

3 Which image on the right is a reflection of the image on the left? Circle the correct letter.

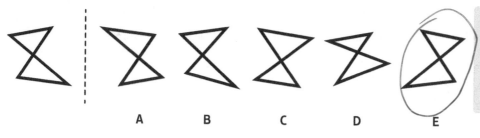

A   B   C   D   E

Compare the **top** half of the images first. You should be able to rule out some options. Then do the same with the **bottom** half of the images to find the answer.

4 Which image on the right is a reflection of the image on the left? Circle the correct letter.

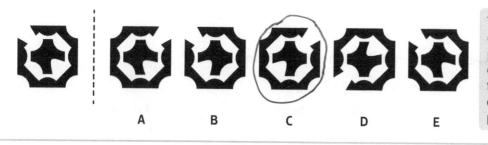

A   B   C   D   E

These shapes look complicated, but don't panic! Ignore the small details and look for parts that are easy to spot. Work out which way each shape points.

Have a go

1 Which image on the right is a reflection of the image on the left? Circle the correct letter.

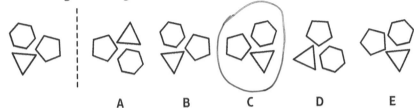

A   B   C   D   E

1 mark

2 Which image on the right is a reflection of the image on the left? Circle the correct letter.

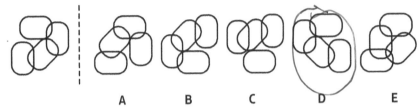

A   B   C   D   E

1 mark

3 Which image on the right is a reflection of the image on the left? Circle the correct letter.

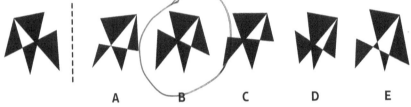

A   B   C   D   E

1 mark

> Compare the answer images. Look for something that is different in all of them. Find the image that shows a reflection of the same part in the image on the left.

4 Which image on the right is a reflection of the image on the left? Circle the correct letter.

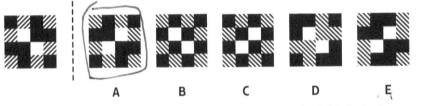

A   B   C   D   E

1 mark

> **123** In questions with grids, use the grid to help you to find the correct answer. The first column of squares in the image on the left has the same pattern as the last column of squares in the correct answer. If you can see a pattern in the squares, make sure the pattern is reflected too.

5 Which image on the right is a reflection of the image on the left? Circle the correct letter.

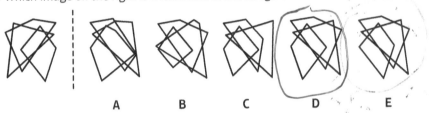

A   B   C   D   E

1 mark

Time to reflect

Mark your *Have a go* section out of 5. How are you doing so far?

Check your answers in the back of the book and see how you are doing.

☐ **Had a go** 0–2 marks	☐ **Nearly there** 3–4 marks	✓ **Nailed it!** 5 marks
Have another look at the *Worked example* on page 8. Then try these questions again.	Look at your incorrect answers. Make sure you understand how to get the correct answer.	Congratulations! Now see whether you can get full marks on the *Timed practice*.

When you are ready, try the *Timed practice* on the next page.

Timed practice

1 Which image on the right is a reflection of the image on the left? Circle the correct letter.

A   B   C   D   E

1 mark

2 Which image on the right is a reflection of the image on the left? Circle the correct letter.

A   B   C   D   E

1 mark

3 Which image on the right is a reflection of the image on the left? Circle the correct letter.

A   B   C   D   E

1 mark

4 Which image on the right is a reflection of the image on the left? Circle the correct letter.

A   B   C   D   E

1 mark

5 Which image on the right is a reflection of the image on the left? Circle the correct letter.

    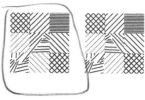

A   B   C   D   E

1 mark

Time to reflect

Mark your *Timed practice* section out of 5. How did you do?

Check your answers in the back of the book and write your score in the progress chart.

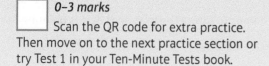

☐ *0–3 marks*
   Scan the QR code for extra practice.
Then move on to the next practice section or
try Test 1 in your Ten-Minute Tests book.

☑ *4–5 marks*
   Well done!
Move on to the next practice section or try
Test 1 in your Ten-Minute Tests book.

2 Rotation

In each of these questions, find which of the five images on the right is a rotation of the image on the left.

1 Which image on the right is a rotation of the image on the left? Circle the correct letter.

A   B   C   D   E

You can cross out the incorrect ones straight away by playing 'spot the difference' with the original picture.

123 **Rotation** means turning an object around a point. The rotation could be clockwise or anticlockwise. The shape and size of the object don't change, but its position might.

1 It cannot be A because the arrow is pointing away from the circle.

2 B must be wrong because the arrow is a different size.

3 C must be wrong because the square has changed shape.

4 In E, the square overlaps the circle too much.

1 Which image on the right is a rotation of the image on the left? Circle the correct letter.

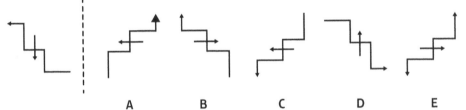

A   B   C   D   E

You could draw the shape and then rotate it.

1 A is wrong because the top arrowhead is too big.

2 C is wrong because the short arrow points the wrong way.

3 E is wrong because it has three arrowheads.

4 Decide whether B or D is right.

2 Which image on the right is a rotation of the image on the left? Circle the correct letter.

5C
D6

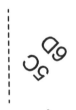

A   B   C   D   E

The image reads '5C D6', so the rotated image needs to read '5C D6' too.

B has been reflected before being rotated, so it must be wrong.

Find a map of your local area. See if you can use landmarks or street names to rotate the map so that it is pointing in the same direction as you.

Guided question

1 Which image on the right is a rotation of the image on the left? Circle the correct letter.

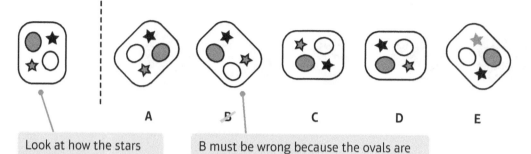

A   B   C   D   E

Look at how the stars line up with the ovals.

B must be wrong because the ovals are both on the same side.

Have a go

1 Which image on the right is a rotation of the image on the left? Circle the correct letter.

Cross out any images with obvious differences first.

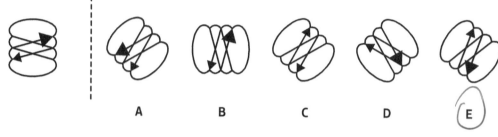

A   B   C   D   E

1 mark

2 Which image on the right is a rotation of the image on the left? Circle the correct letter.

When shapes overlap, make sure the right ones are on top of each other in the answer image.

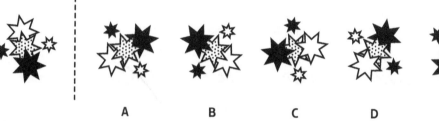

A   B   C   D   E

1 mark

3 Which image on the right is a rotation of the image on the left? Circle the correct letter.

For more complex images, it can be helpful to count the features of the shapes, such as the number of corners or sides.

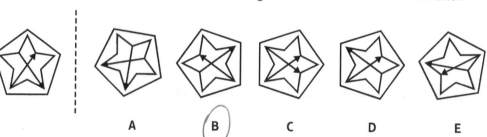

A   B   C   D   E

1 mark

Beyond the exam

Draw a simple image, rotate it 90° and then copy it on another piece of paper. Rotate it twice more by 90°, copying it each time. Compare each drawing with your original image.

Have a go

1 Which image on the right is a rotation of the image on the left? Circle the correct letter.

A (B) C D E

1 mark

2 Which image on the right is a rotation of the image on the left? Circle the correct letter.

Make sure you look at the whole image carefully. The answer images might only have very small differences.

A (B) C (D) E

1 mark

3 Which image on the right is a rotation of the image on the left? Circle the correct letter.

Start by looking for differences in shape and size. Cross out any answers that must be wrong.

A B (C) D E

1 mark

4 Which image on the right is a rotation of the image on the left? Circle the correct letter.

Break down complex images into simpler shapes.

A B C D (E)

1 mark

Time to reflect

Mark your *Have a go* section out of 4. How are you doing so far?

Check your answers in the back of the book and see how you are doing.

☐ **Had a go** 0–1 marks	✓ **Nearly there** 2–3 marks	☐ **Nailed it!** 4 marks
Have another look at the *Worked example* on page 12. Then try these questions again.	Look at your incorrect answers. Make sure you understand how to get the correct answer.	Congratulations! Now see whether you can get full marks on the *Timed practice*.

When you are ready, try the *Timed practice* on the next page.

Timed practice

⏱ **4**

🌀 **1** Which image on the right is a rotation of the image on the left? Circle the correct letter.

          A   **B**   **C**   **D**   **E**

1 mark

🌀 **2** Which image on the right is a rotation of the image on the left? Circle the correct letter.

 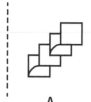   

          A   **B**   **C**   **D**   **E**

1 mark

🌀 **3** Which image on the right is a rotation of the image on the left? Circle the correct letter.

 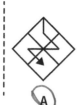   

          A   **B**   **C**   **D**   **E**

1 mark

🌀 **4** Which image on the right is a rotation of the image on the left? Circle the correct letter.

          A   **B**   **C**   **D**   **E**

1 mark

🌀 **5** Which image on the right is a rotation of the image on the left? Circle the correct letter.

          A   **B**   **C**   **D**   **E**

1 mark

Time to reflect

Mark your *Timed practice* section out of 5. How did you do?

Check your answers in the back of the book and write your score in the progress chart.

☐ *0–3 marks*
Scan the QR code for extra practice.
Then move on to the next practice section or
try Test 2 in your Ten-Minute Tests book.

☐ *4–5 marks*
Well done!
Move on to the next practice section or try
Test 2 in your Ten-Minute Tests book.

3 Hidden shapes

In each of these questions, find which of the five images on the right contains the shape on the left. The hidden shape will be inside a more complex image. It will be the same size, but it might be rotated.

Worked example

1 Which image on the right contains the image on the left? Circle the correct letter.

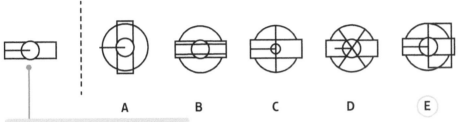

A   B   C   D   E

This image is the hidden shape.

① A is incorrect because the horizontal line sticks out of the rectangle.

② The straight lines do not go through the centre of the circle in B.

③ The circle in C is too small.

④ The horizontal line in the middle of D is too short.

⑤ The answer must be E. The pattern inside matches the image on the left perfectly.

Guided questions

1 Which image on the right contains the image on the left? Circle the correct letter.

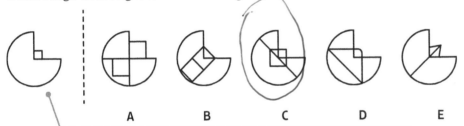

A   B   C   D   E

Break down the image into separate parts. In this question you need to find three-quarters of a circle and a small square.

① Look for the three-quarter circle. It appears in all of the images, so this doesn't help.

② Look for the small square. It is missing from A and B, so these must be incorrect.

2 Which image on the right contains the image on the left? Circle the correct letter.

A   B   C   D   E

The hidden shape is a triangle inside a kite.

① A, C and D have different triangles, so must be incorrect.

② In B and E, look at how the triangle and kite fit together. Compare them with the image on the left.

Beyond the exam

Logos of famous companies and brands often contain hidden images. Take a closer look at some logos to see if you can spot any images that tell you about the company's name or what they do.

Guided questions

1 Which image on the right contains the image on the left? Circle the correct letter.

A   B   C   D   E

The hidden shape has been rotated by 90° clockwise or anticlockwise. Rotated hidden shapes can be harder to spot, so it's important to practise your rotation skills.

① You can see from the outline of the hidden shape that it must have been rotated.

② On a separate piece of paper, sketch the two lines inside the hidden shape.

③ Try rotating them clockwise and anticlockwise.

④ Work out which image matches the curve in the image on the left.

2 Which image on the right contains the image on the left? Circle the correct letter.

A   B   C   D   E

Look at the oval to see how it has rotated, and then see if the curved line has rotated in the same way.

B is incorrect because the line crosses through the oval diagonally.

E is incorrect because there aren't any curved lines through the oval.

Have a go

1 Which image on the right contains the image on the left? Circle the correct letter.

Remember the shape will not have been reflected, but it might have been rotated.

A   B   C   D   E

1 mark

2 Which image on the right contains the image on the left? Circle the correct letter.

If you are looking for a pattern inside a larger shape, use the large shape to help. For example, think about whether the pattern goes right to the edges of the large shape.

A   B   C   D   E

1 mark

Have a go

1 Which image on the right contains the image on the left? Circle the correct letter.

  A   B   C   D   E

1 mark

2 Which image on the right contains the image on the left? Circle the correct letter.

 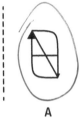

  A   B   C   D   E

1 mark

> Start by looking for things that are easy to spot, such as whether parts of the hidden shape are the right size.

3 Which image on the right contains the image on the left? Circle the correct letter.

  A   B   C   D   E

1 mark

4 Which image on the right contains the image on the left? Circle the correct letter.

 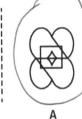

  A   B   C   D   E

1 mark

> Break down the image into smaller parts and look for each part separately.

Time to reflect

Mark your *Have a go* section out of 4. How are you doing so far?

Check your answers in the back of the book and see how you are doing.

☐ **Had a go**	☐ **Nearly there**	☑ **Nailed it!**
0–1 marks	*2–3 marks*	*4 marks*
Have another look at the *Worked example* on page 16. Then try these questions again.	Look at your incorrect answers. Make sure you understand how to get the correct answer.	Congratulations! Now see whether you can get full marks on the *Timed practice*.

When you are ready, try the *Timed practice* on the next page.

Timed practice

4

1 Which image on the right contains the image on the left? Circle the correct letter.

   A   B   C   D   E

1 mark

2 Which image on the right contains the image on the left? Circle the correct letter.

   A   B   C   D   E

1 mark

3 Which image on the right contains the image on the left? Circle the correct letter.

   A   B   C   D   E

1 mark

4 Which image on the right contains the image on the left? Circle the correct letter.

   A   B   C   D   E

1 mark

5 Which image on the right contains the image on the left? Circle the correct letter.

   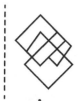   

   A   B   C   D   E

1 mark

Time to reflect

Mark your *Timed practice* section out of 5. How did you do?
Check your answers in the back of the book and write your score in the progress chart.

☐ *0–3 marks*
  Scan the QR code for extra practice.
Then move on to the next practice section or
try Test 3 in your Ten-Minute Tests book.

☑ *4–5 marks*
  Well done!
Move on to the next practice section or try
Test 3 in your Ten-Minute Tests book.

4 Odd one out

Images can have many differences, for example size, shape, number of parts, colour, rotation or reflection. In each of these questions, find the image that is most different from all the others.

Worked example

1 Which image is least like the others? Circle the correct letter.

A   B   C   D   E

> Find a shape or pattern that is used in all the images, but is different in one. Look for all the differences between the images and rule them out one by one.

1 Try counting the stars. Each image has three stars, so the number of stars isn't the important change.

2 Look at where the stars are. B has two stars at the top and one at the bottom, so it is different from A, C and D. But it is similar to image E, which also has two stars at the top and one at the bottom.

3 Look at the colour of the stars. C has two white stars, and the rest only have one. So C is the odd one out.

Guided questions

1 Which image is least like the others? Circle the correct letter.

         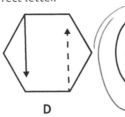

A   B   C   D   E

1 Look at the outer shapes. They are all different and they can't all be the odd one out!

2 Look at the direction of the arrows. A and B are similar because the arrows cross over. C, D and E are similar because the arrows are parallel.

3 Look at the style of the arrows to find the odd one out.

> Look for differences between the arrows. Try looking at line styles, colours, whether they point up or down and whether they go clockwise or anticlockwise.

2 Which image is least like the others? Circle the correct letter.

A   B   C   D   E

> **123** Clockwise is the direction the hands move around a clock. Anticlockwise is the opposite direction. clockwise anticlockwise

Beyond the exam

Think of five animals or objects and make a list of as many similarities and differences as you can in one minute. For example, crayons are similar to parrots because they are colourful, but different because crayons can't talk.

Guided questions

1 Which image is least like the others? Circle the correct letter.

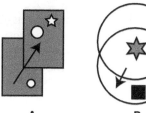 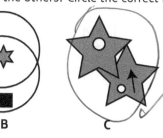 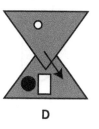 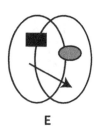

A   B   C   D   E

There are a lot of small details in these images, so look at them one at a time to begin with. Something is different about the arrow in one of the images.

2 Which image is least like the others? Circle the correct letter.

A   B   C   D   E

Four of these images are rotations of each other. Look closely at the rectangle to find the odd one out.

Have a go

1 Which image is least like the others? Circle the correct letter.

 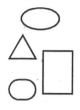  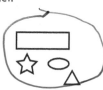 

A   B   C   D   E

1 mark

Look closely at the shape that is in all five images.

2 Which image is least like the others? Circle the correct letter.

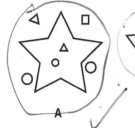    

A   B   C   D   E

1 mark

Have a go

1 Which image is least like the others? Circle the correct letter.

A   B   C   D   E

You don't need to pay attention to every detail in the images. Focus on the parts that change.

1 mark

2 Which image is least like the others? Circle the correct letter.

A   B   C   D   E

You can rule out any parts that are identical in all the images.

1 mark

3 Which image is least like the others? Circle the correct letter.

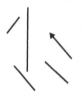    

A   B   C   D   E

1 mark

4 Which image is least like the others? Circle the correct letter.

   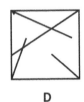

A   B   C   D   E

1 mark

Time to reflect

Mark your *Have a go* section out of 4. How are you doing so far?

Check your answers in the back of the book and see how you are doing.

	Had a go		**Nearly there**	✓	**Nailed it!**
	0–1 marks		*2–3 marks*		*4 marks*

Had a go
0–1 marks
Have another look at the *Worked example* on page 20. Then try these questions again.

Nearly there
2–3 marks
Look at your incorrect answers. Make sure you understand how to get the correct answer.

Nailed it!
4 marks
Congratulations! Now see whether you can get full marks on the *Timed practice*.

When you are ready, try the *Timed practice* on the next page.

Timed practice

4

1 Which image is least like the others? Circle the correct letter.

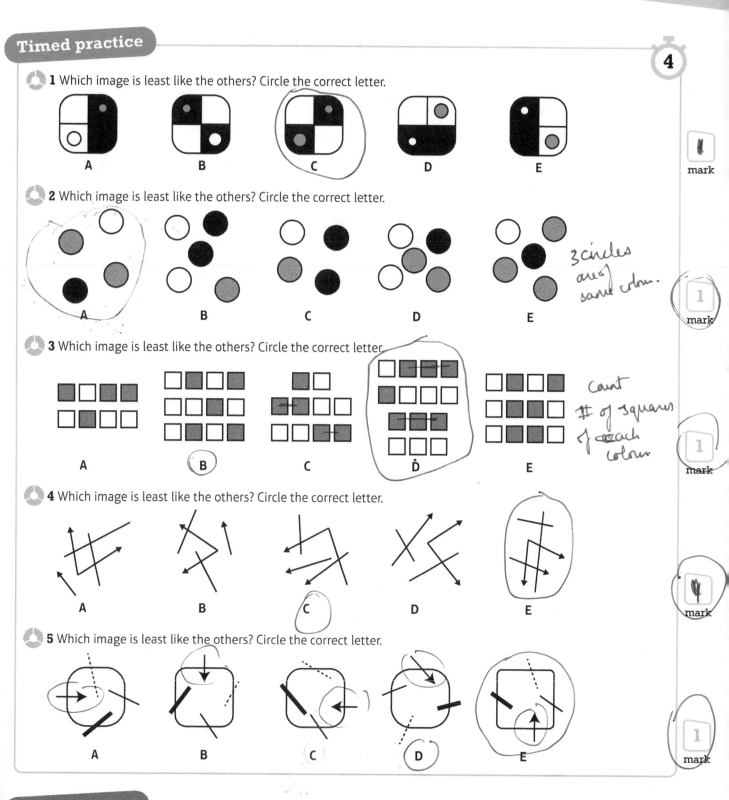

A   B   C   D   E

1 mark

2 Which image is least like the others? Circle the correct letter.

A   B   C   D   E

3 circles are same colour.

1 mark

3 Which image is least like the others? Circle the correct letter.

A   B   C   D   E

Count # of squares of each colour

1 mark

4 Which image is least like the others? Circle the correct letter.

A   B   C   D   E

1 mark

5 Which image is least like the others? Circle the correct letter.

A   B   C   D   E

1 mark

Time to reflect

Mark your *Timed practice* section out of 5. How did you do?
Check your answers in the back of the book and write your score in the progress chart.

☐ *0–3 marks*
 Scan the QR code for extra practice.
Then move on to the next practice section or
try Test 4 in your Ten-Minute Tests book.

✓ *4–5 marks*
 Well done!
Move on to the next practice section or try
Test 4 in your Ten-Minute Tests book.

5 Which image belongs?

In each of these questions, find which image on the right belongs with the images on the left. All the images are similar in some way, but you need to find the one that is most similar.

Worked example

1 Which image on the right is most similar to the two images on the left? Circle the correct letter.

A   B   C   D   E

> Look for features that the images on the left share, and find the image on the right that has the most in common with them. This could include colour, number of sides, shape and lines of symmetry.

1 Both images on the left are triangles. A is probably wrong because it has four sides.

2 The images on the left have vertical symmetry. C and D do not, so these are unlikely to be the answer. B and E are most likely to be correct.

3 The triangles on the left have a horizontal side at the top. Only E matches them in this way. E also has a line of symmetry down the middle, so E is the most similar to the images on the left.

Guided questions

1 Which image on the right is most similar to the two images on the left? Circle the correct letter.

A   B   C   D   E

> Both images on the left are divided equally into six shapes, three of which are grey.

1 A and C have three grey shapes.

2 A, B, C and D are divided into six shapes.

3 B, C and D are divided into six **identical** shapes.

4 Find the image with the most features in common with the images on the left.

2 Which image on the right is most similar to the two images on the left? Circle the correct letter.

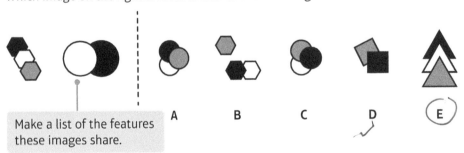

Make a list of the features these images share.

A   B   C   D   E

1 Both images have a white shape and a black shape.

2 Both images are made up of a row of identical, overlapping shapes.

3 In both images, the white shape overlaps on top of the black shape.

4 Look for the image on the right that has all these features.

Guided questions

1 Which image on the right is most similar to the two images on the left? Circle the correct letter.

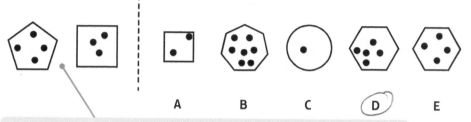

A　　B　　C　　D　　E

Find a connection between the number of dots and the number of sides.

2 Which image on the right is most similar to the three images on the left? Circle the correct letter.

Look at how the shapes overlap.

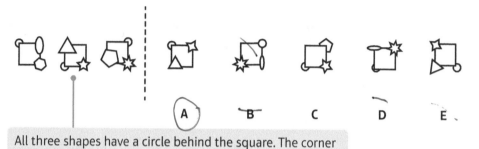

A　　B　　C　　D　　E

All three shapes have a circle behind the square. The corner of the square is always in the centre of the circle.

Have a go

1 Which image on the right is most similar to the two images on the left? Circle the correct letter.

Look at the position of each part of the image.

A　　B　　C　　D　　E

1 mark

2 Which image on the right is most similar to the two images on the left? Circle the correct letter.

Think about symmetry and parallel lines.

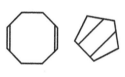 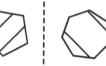 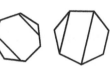

A　　B　　C　　D　　E

123 Parallel lines always stay the same distance apart and never touch.

1 mark

Have a go

1 Which image on the right is most similar to the two images on the left? Circle the correct letter.

(A)   B   C   D   E

> Finding one or two similarities might not be enough. You need to find the **most** similar option.

 1 mark

2 Which image on the right is most similar to the three images on the left? Circle the correct letter.

A   B   (C)   D   E

> Some features are the same in every image. Focus on the details that change.

1 mark

3 Which image on the right is most similar to the three images on the left? Circle the correct letter.

A   B   C   (D)   E

> Pay attention to the lines inside the shapes.

1 mark

4 Which image on the right is most similar to the three images on the left? Circle the correct letter.

A   B   (C)   D   E

> Think about the positions of the smaller shapes in each image.

mark

Time to reflect

Mark your *Have a go* section out of 4. How are you doing so far?

Check your answers in the back of the book and see how you are doing.

☐ **Had a go**	☐ **Nearly there**	☐ **Nailed it!**
0–1 marks	*2–3 marks*	*4 marks*
Have another look at the *Worked example* on page 24. Then try these questions again.	Look at your incorrect answers. Make sure you understand how to get the correct answer.	Congratulations! Now see whether you can get full marks on the timed practice.

When you are ready, try the *Timed practice* on the next page.

Timed practice

④

1 Which image on the right is most similar to the two images on the left? Circle the correct letter.

        A   B   C   (D)   E

mark

2 Which image on the right is most similar to the two images on the left? Circle the correct letter.

        A   B   C   (D)   E

1
mark

3 Which image on the right is most similar to the two images on the left? Circle the correct letter.

        A   B   (C)   D   E

1
mark

4 Which image on the right is most similar to the two images on the left? Circle the correct letter.

        A   B   C   (D)   E

1
mark

5 Which image on the right is most similar to the three images on the left? Circle the correct letter.

        A   B   C   (D)   E

1
mark

Time to reflect

Mark your *Timed practice* section out of 5. How did you do?

Check your answers in the back of the book and write your score in the progress chart.

☐ *0–3 marks*
    Scan the QR code for extra practice.
Then move on to the next practice section or
try Test 6 in your Ten-Minute Tests book.

☐ *4–5 marks*
    Well done!
Move on to the next practice section or try
Test 6 in your Ten-Minute Tests book.

Checkpoint 1

In this checkpoint you will practise skills from the **Transformations** and **Similarities and differences** topics.

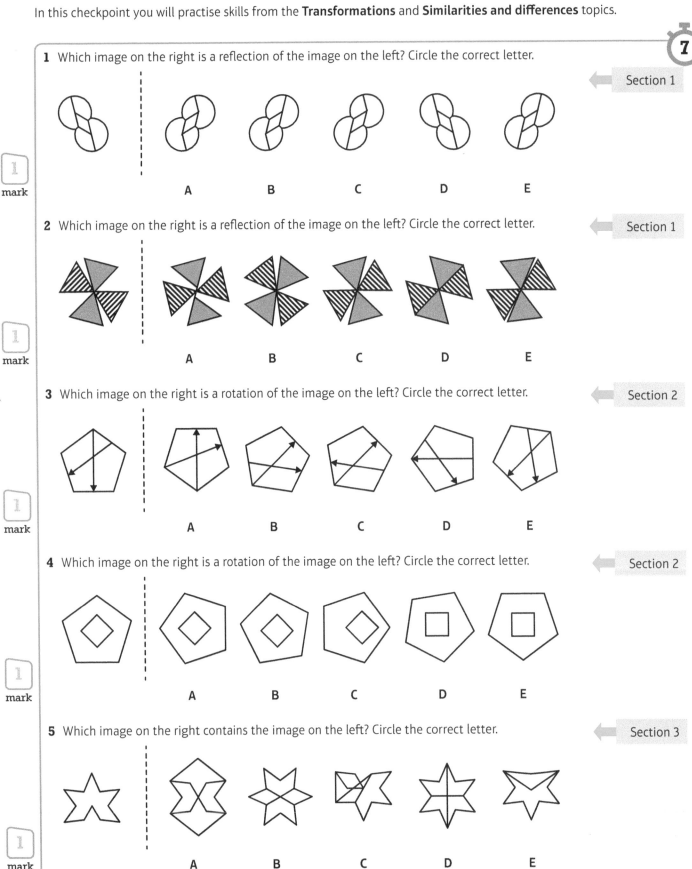

1 Which image on the right is a reflection of the image on the left? Circle the correct letter.

Section 1

1 mark

A   B   C   D   E

2 Which image on the right is a reflection of the image on the left? Circle the correct letter.

Section 1

1 mark

A   B   C   D   E

3 Which image on the right is a rotation of the image on the left? Circle the correct letter.

Section 2

1 mark

A   B   C   D   E

4 Which image on the right is a rotation of the image on the left? Circle the correct letter.

Section 2

1 mark

A   B   C   D   E

5 Which image on the right contains the image on the left? Circle the correct letter.

Section 3

1 mark

A   B   C   D   E

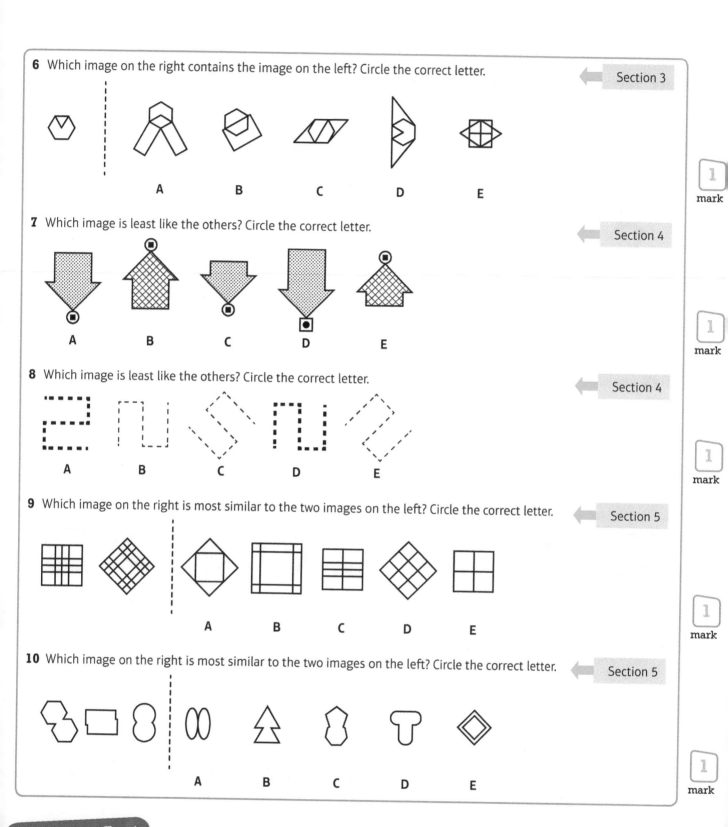

6 Which image on the right contains the image on the left? Circle the correct letter.

Section 3

A   B   C   D   E

1 mark

7 Which image is least like the others? Circle the correct letter.

Section 4

A   B   C   D   E

1 mark

8 Which image is least like the others? Circle the correct letter.

Section 4

A   B   C   D   E

1 mark

9 Which image on the right is most similar to the two images on the left? Circle the correct letter.

Section 5

A   B   C   D   E

1 mark

10 Which image on the right is most similar to the two images on the left? Circle the correct letter.

Section 5

A   B   C   D   E

1 mark

Time to reflect

Mark your *Checkpoint* out of 10. How did you do?

1 Check your answers in the back of the book and write your score in the progress chart. If any of your answers are incorrect, use the section links to find out which practice sections to look at again.

2 Scan the QR code for extra practice.

3 Move on to the next practice section.

6 Complete the pair

In each of these questions, find which image on the right completes the pair in the same way as the first pair. Work out what changes take place between images in the first pair. Then work out what the third image would look like if you changed it in the same way.

Worked example

1 Which image on the right completes the second pair in the same way as the first pair? Circle the correct letter.

A   B   C   D   E

Work out what changes the first image into the second image.

Imagine this image changing in the same way. Work out which of the answer options it would change into.

The white parts of the star shape disappear. The black parts become white.

1 The shapes of A and E are correct, but the colours haven't changed.

2 C and D are the wrong shape.

3 B must be correct, because the white parts of the star have disappeared and the black parts have turned white.

Guided questions

1 Which image on the right completes the second pair in the same way as the first pair? Circle the correct letter.

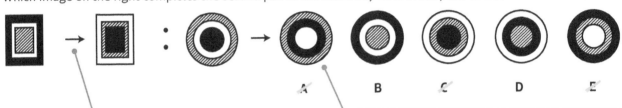

A   B   C   D   E

The rectangles change colour. The shading of the biggest rectangle becomes the shading of the smallest rectangle, and the other two colours move outwards.

The correct answer must have a shaded circle in the middle. Cross out A, C and E and work out which circle should be black and which circle should be white.

2 Which image on the right completes the second pair in the same way as the first pair? Circle the correct letter.

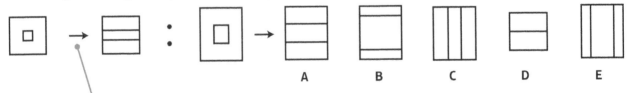

A   B   C   D   E

The inner shape is replaced with two horizontal lines. This means the images with vertical lines must be wrong.

Look for similarities between the inner shape in the first image and the horizontal lines in the second image.

Beyond the exam

Draw two similar shapes on separate pieces of paper. Give one to a friend and keep the other one hidden. Explain the differences between the two shapes to your friend and challenge them to draw the hidden shape.

Guided questions

1 Which image on the right completes the second pair in the same way as the first pair? Circle the correct letter.

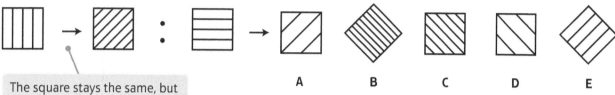

The square stays the same, but the stripes inside it change.

A   B   C   D   E

① The square changes in B and E, so they must be wrong.

② Look closely at how the stripes change.

2 Which image on the right completes the second pair in the same way as the first pair? Circle the correct letter.

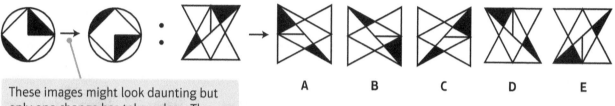

These images might look daunting but only one change has taken place. The image has been rotated.

A   B   C   D   E

Have a go

1 Which image on the right completes the second pair in the same way as the first pair? Circle the correct letter.

Sometimes a reflection looks the same as a rotation. You might need to look at the answer images to decide whether the image has been rotated or reflected.

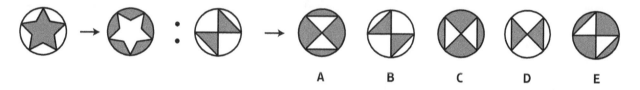

A   B   C   D   E

1 mark

2 Which image on the right completes the second pair in the same way as the first pair? Circle the correct letter.

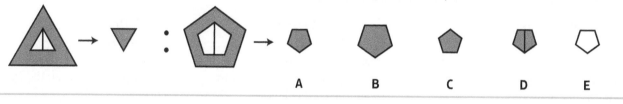

A   B   C   D   E

1 mark

Linear sequences

Complete the pair

Have a go

1 Which image on the right completes the second pair in the same way as the first pair? Circle the correct letter.

Think carefully about whether the shape has been rotated or reflected.

1 mark

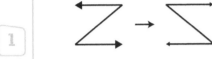 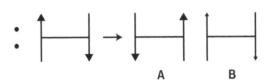 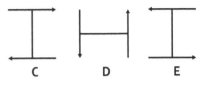

A   B   C   D   E

2 Which image on the right completes the second pair in the same way as the first pair? Circle the correct letter.

1 mark

   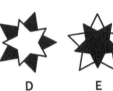

A   B   C   D   E

3 Which image on the right completes the second pair in the same way as the first pair? Circle the correct letter.

1 mark

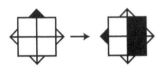 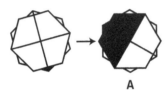 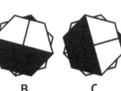 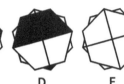

A   B   C   D   E

4 Which image on the right completes the second pair in the same way as the first pair? Circle the correct letter.

1 mark

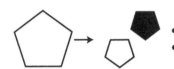 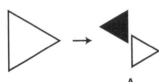

A   B   C   D   E

Time to reflect

Mark your *Have a go* section out of 4. How are you doing so far?

Check your answers in the back of the book and see how you are doing.

Had a go	**Nearly there**	**Nailed it!**
0–1 marks	2–3 marks	4 marks
Have another look at the *Worked example* on page 30. Then try these questions again.	Look at your incorrect answers. Make sure you understand how to get the correct answer.	Congratulations! Now see whether you can get full marks on the *Timed practice*.

When you are ready, try the *Timed practice* on the next page.

Timed practice

④

1 Which image on the right completes the second pair in the same way as the first pair? Circle the correct letter.

A B C D E

1 mark

2 Which image on the right completes the second pair in the same way as the first pair? Circle the correct letter.

A B C D E

1 mark

3 Which image on the right completes the second pair in the same way as the first pair? Circle the correct letter.

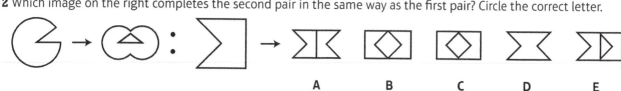

A B C D E

1 mark

4 Which image on the right completes the second pair in the same way as the first pair? Circle the correct letter.

A B C D E

1 mark

5 Which image on the right completes the second pair in the same way as the first pair? Circle the correct letter.

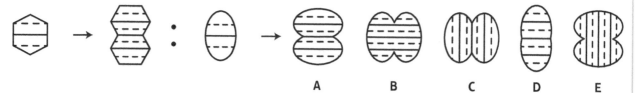

A B C D E

1 mark

Time to reflect

Mark your *Timed practice* section out of 5. How did you do?
Check your answers in the back of the book and write your score in the progress chart.

☐ *0–3 marks*
Scan the QR code for extra practice.
Then move on to the next practice section or try Test 8 in your Ten-Minute Tests book.

☐ *4–5 marks*
Well done!
Move on to the next practice section or try Test 8 in your Ten-Minute Tests book.

7 Complete the series

Each of these questions shows a series of images with one image missing. Find which of the images on the right completes the series.

Worked example

1 Which image on the right is missing from the series? Circle the correct letter.

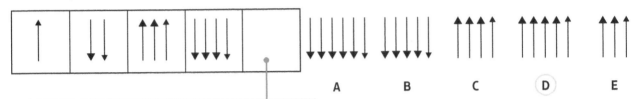

A   B   C   D   E

'Read' the series from left to right. Work out what the pattern is by finding what changes in each image.

1 An extra arrow is added in each image. The correct answer must have five arrows. You can cross out A, C and E.

2 At each step the arrows switch direction, so the arrows in the missing image have to point up. You can cross out B.

3 D must be the correct answer.

Guided questions

1 Which image on the right is missing from the series? Circle the correct letter.

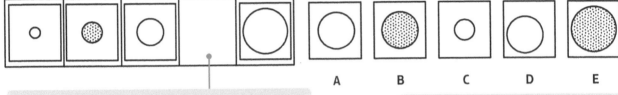

A   B   C   D   E

The empty space can appear anywhere in the series. It does not have to be at the end.

abc 'Alternating' means taking turns.

1 Look for alternating patterns. The first, third and fifth circles are white, but the second circle is dotted. So, odd images are white and even images are dotted. Use this to work out the colour of the missing fourth image.

2 Look for something else that changes at each step to help you find the answer.

2 Which image on the right is missing from the series? Circle the correct letter.

The images have three different parts that change each time. Look at the chain of squares, the chain of circles and the chain of triangles separately.

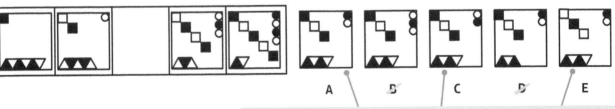

A   B   C   D   E

These three images have the right number of triangles, squares and circles. Use the colours to decide which is correct.

1 Which image on the right is missing from the series? Circle the correct letter.

A   B   C   D   E

1 Work out which side of the circle should have a slice cut out of it.

2 Decide how big the slice should be.

2 Which image on the right is missing from the series? Circle the correct letter.

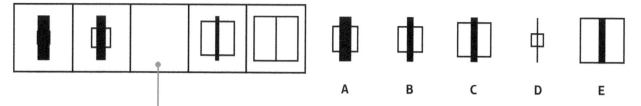

A   B   C   D   E

Compare these images to work out the series pattern.
Then apply this pattern to the missing image.

1 Which image on the right is missing from the series? Circle the correct letter.

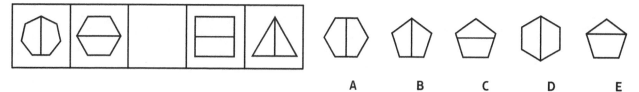

A   B   C   D   E

1 mark

2 Which image on the right is missing from the series? Circle the correct letter.

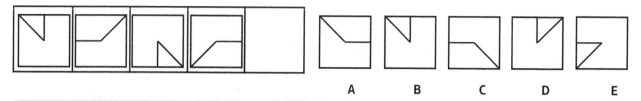

A   B   C   D   E

1 mark

Try drawing what you think the answer will be first.
See if it matches one of the answer images.

Make sequence patterns using playing cards. You could alternate the suit, the colour or odd and even numbers, or think of something more complex. Think about what needs to change or stay the same on each card in order to make a pattern.

Have a go

1 Which image on the right is missing from the series? Circle the correct letter.

1 mark

A   B   C   D   E

If the empty space is near the start of the series, try 'reading' the series backwards, from right to left.

2 Which image on the right is missing from the series? Circle the correct letter.

1 mark

A   B   C   D   E

3 Which image on the right is missing from the series? Circle the correct letter.

1 mark

A   B   C   D   E

4 Which image on the right is missing from the series? Circle the correct letter.

Break down complex images into simpler shapes. Look at each shape on its own.

1 mark

A   B   C   D   E

Time to reflect

Mark your *Have a go* section out of 4. How are you doing so far?

Check your answers in the back of the book and see how you are doing.

Had a go
0–1 marks
Have another look at the *Worked example* on page 34. Then try these questions again.

Nearly there
2–3 marks
Look at your incorrect answers. Make sure you understand how to get the correct answer.

Nailed it!
4 marks
Congratulations! Now see whether you can get full marks on the *Timed practice*.

When you are ready, try the *Timed practice* on the next page.

Timed practice

4

1 Which image on the right is missing from the series? Circle the correct letter.

A B C D E

1 mark

2 Which image on the right is missing from the series? Circle the correct letter.

A B C D E

1 mark

3 Which image on the right is missing from the series? Circle the correct letter.

A B C D E

1 mark

4 Which image on the right is missing from the series? Circle the correct letter.

A B C D E

1 mark

5 Which image on the right is missing from the series? Circle the correct letter.

A B C D E

1 mark

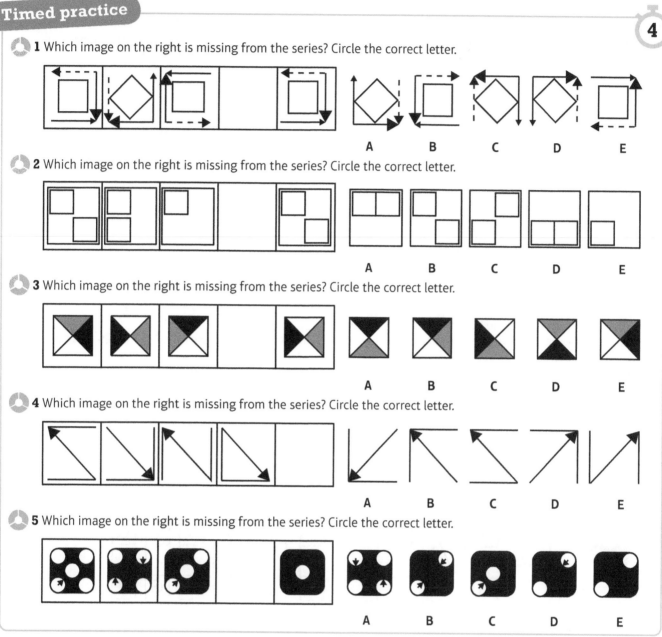

Time to reflect

Mark your *Timed practice* section out of 5. How did you do?

Check your answers in the back of the book and write your score in the progress chart.

	0–3 marks

Scan the QR code for extra practice.
Then move on to the next practice section or
try Test 9 in your Ten-Minute Tests book.

	4–5 marks

Well done!
Move on to the next practice section or try
Test 9 in your Ten-Minute Tests book.

8 Codes in boxes

In each of these questions, find which code on the right matches the image in the box at the end of the question. Each letter of the code tells you about one feature of the image. You need to work out what the code for the final image should be.

1 Which code matches the final image? Circle the correct letter.

Look for repeated letters. These codes both have P in the top box. The only similarity between the images is that they both have circles. So the top box must show the type of shape and P must mean circle.

The top letter in each code tells you a different type of information from the bottom letter.

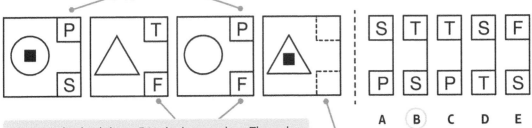

These codes both have F in the bottom box. The only similarity between the images is that they don't have a black square. So the bottom letter tells you whether there is a black square. S means there is a black square and F means there isn't.

This image is a triangle so the top letter is T. It has a black square so the bottom letter is S.

The letters don't stand for anything. For example, T won't always mean a triangle.

1 Which code matches the final image? Circle the correct letter.

In this question, the colour isn't important. You can tell because some top letters and some bottom letters are repeated, but no colours are repeated.

    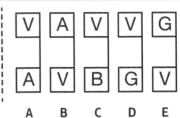

A   B   C   D   E

① The first two images both have A in the top box. They are both hearts, and have nothing else in common. So A means heart and the top letter of each image must tell you the shape.

② The question image has the same droplet shape as the third image, so it must have the same top letter.

③ The shapes are different sizes. Look for similarities between the sizes of the shapes to help you work out the bottom letter.

2 Which code matches the final image? Circle the correct letter.

    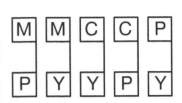

A   B   C   D   E

All the images have a six-sided shape, but the shapes are at different angles. P means there are angles at the top and bottom of the shape. Y means there are straight lines at the top and bottom of the shape. The bottom letter of the missing code must be Y.

Look at the number of lines inside the shape to work out what the top letter tells you.

Guided questions

1 Which code matches the final image? Circle the correct letter.

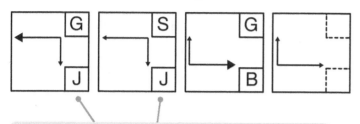

A   B   C   D   E

Think about the arrow size and the way the arrows point.

These codes share the letter J. Look for similarities between the images to help you decide what J means.

2 Which code matches the final image? Circle the correct letter.

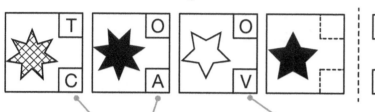

A   B   C   D   E

Look at the orientation of the stars. Some stand on one point and some on two points.

These two stars have the same number of points, but the codes don't have any letters in common. This means there isn't a letter that tells you the number of points.

All the bottom letters are different, so find something that is different in all the images.

Have a go

1 Which code matches the final image? Circle the correct letter.

A code might show whether or not a particular feature is in the image.

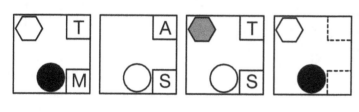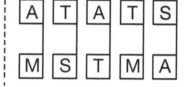

A   B   C   D   E

1 mark

2 Which code matches the final image? Circle the correct letter.

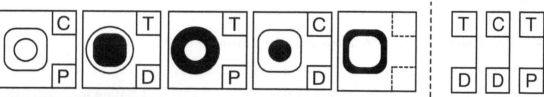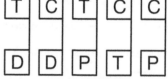

A   B   C   D   E

1 mark

If lots of features change, think about each one separately.

Have a go

1 Which code matches the final image? Circle the correct letter.

If there are more variations of a feature than there are letters in the code, it cannot be part of the code.

O		L		O		O	
	K		K		B		

O	L	B	L	O
B	B	L	K	K
A	B	C	D	E

1 mark

2 Which code matches the final image? Circle the correct letter.

Z		Q		Q			
	O		T		O		

Q	T	Z	Z	Q
R	T	T	O	O
A	B	C	D	E

1 mark

3 Which code matches the final image? Circle the correct letter.

Break down complex images into simple shapes.

H		P		H			
	I		A		A		

P	H	H	P	P
I	P	A	A	H
A	B	C	D	E

1 mark

4 Which code matches the final image? Circle the correct letter.

You don't have to start with the top letter in a code. If the bottom row has lots of repeated letters, it might be easier to start there.

B		P		R		B			
	G		N		G		N		

R	P	B	P	R
G	G	N	N	N
A	B	C	D	E

1 mark

Time to reflect

Mark your *Have a go* section out of 4. How are you doing so far?

Check your answers in the back of the book and see how you are doing.

Had a go
0–1 marks
Have another look at the *Worked example* on page 38. Then try these questions again.

Nearly there
2–3 marks
Look at your incorrect answers. Make sure you understand how to get the correct answer.

Nailed it!
4 marks
Congratulations! Now see whether you can get full marks on the *Timed practice.*

When you are ready, try the *Timed practice* on the next page.

Timed practice

4

1 Which code matches the final image? Circle the correct letter.

U	L	U	L	A
A	V	V	A	U
A	B	C	D	E

1 mark

2 Which code matches the final image? Circle the correct letter.

R	W	W	R	M
D	D	T	T	D
A	B	C	D	E

1 mark

3 Which code matches the final image? Circle the correct letter.

O	D	O	O	D
D	T	F	T	F
A	B	C	D	E

1 mark

4 Which code matches the final image? Circle the correct letter.

U	K	K	U	E
K	U	E	V	V
A	B	C	D	E

1 mark

5 Which code matches the final image? Circle the correct letter.

K	K	D	D	D
I	X	H	I	X
A	B	C	D	E

1 mark

Time to reflect

Mark your *Timed practice* section out of 5. How did you do?

Check your answers in the back of the book and write your score in the progress chart.

0–3 marks

Scan the QR code for extra practice.
Then move on to the next practice section or
try Test 12 in your Ten-Minute Tests book.

4–5 marks

Well done!
Move on to the next practice section or try
Test 12 in your Ten-Minute Tests book.

9 Codes in lists

Each of these questions shows you a list of images. Each image has a code underneath, apart from the final one. Each letter of the code tells you about one feature of the image. You need to work out what the code for the final image should be.

Worked example

1 Which code matches the final image? Circle the correct letter.

The letters in the codes don't stand for anything. For example, B doesn't necessarily mean black.

Look for a letter that is the same in two of the codes. Then look for something that is the same in those two images to work out what the letter represents.

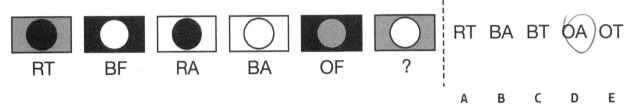

| BZ | BT | PT | FZ | PN | ? |

NB FT BN PZ FN

A B C D (E)

These codes start with B. Both shapes are rectangles. So B means a rectangle. The first letter in these codes tells you the shape.

These codes end with T. They are both white. So T means white. The second letter in these codes tells you the colour of the shape.

This image is the same shape as FZ, so the shape letter is F. It is the same colour as PN, so the colour letter is N. The answer is FN.

Guided questions

1 Which code matches the final image? Circle the correct letter.

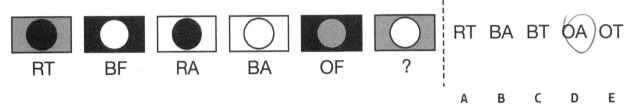

| RT | BF | RA | BA | OF | ? |

RT BA BT (OA) OT

A B C D E

1 Two of the codes start with R. Both of these images have black circles.

2 If R means a black circle, the first letter of every code tells you the colour of the circle. Find a circle that matches the final image to work out the first letter of the answer code.

3 Find two images with the same second letter. Look at what the images have in common. Then use this to work out the second letter of the answer code.

2 Which code matches the final image? Circle the correct letter.

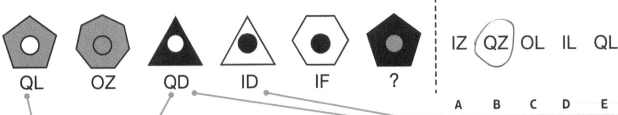

| QL | OZ | QD | ID | IF | ? |

IZ (QZ) OL IL QL

A B C D E

Both of these codes have Q as the first letter. The only similarity is that both images have a white circle inside. So the first letter of the code is the colour of the circle. The question image has a grey circle. Find a shape with a grey circle and use it to work out the first letter of the code.

Both of these codes have D as the second letter. The only similarity is that both images are triangles. So the second letter of the code is the type of shape. The question image has five sides. Find a shape with five sides and use it to work out the second letter of the code.

Guided questions

1 Which code matches the final image? Circle the correct letter.

ZW, ZK and ZS all have Z as the first letter. Find a similarity between these images.

ZW   JS   ZK   ZS   JW   ?

ZS   JW   JK   ZW   JS

A   B   C   D   E

The black circle in the middle of some of the images isn't important here. You can tell this isn't what Z means, because ZS doesn't have the same circle as ZW and ZK.

2 Which code matches the final image? Circle the correct letter.

RP   RE   SK   RU   SU   ?

RU   SU   SE   RK   SP

A   B   C   D   E

Use the dotted lines to work out the first letter, then look for other similarities and differences to work out the second letter.

Have a go

1 Which code matches the final image? Circle the correct letter.

A letter might tell you whether a particular feature is in the image or not.

DW   OV   DV   DJ   OW   ?

OV   DJ   OW   DV   OJ

A   B   C   D   E

1 mark

2 Which code matches the final image? Circle the correct letter.

Remember that there is a new code for each question. Codes for previous questions won't help you.

When you have worked out one letter, write it down to help you remember.

CA   HX   CE   HU   RX   ?

RA   CX   HU   RE   HA

A   B   C   D   E

1 mark

Have a go

1 Which code matches the final image? Circle the correct letter.

> Not everything in the images has a code letter. You might need to ignore some distractions.

1 mark

TL   MC   TG   ML   QC   ?

TL QG MG TC QL

A   B   C   D   E

2 Which code matches the final image? Circle the correct letter.

> One letter might tell you about two things at once, such as size and direction.

1 mark

NV   SC   NO   PV   SX   ?

PC SO PX NC SV

A   B   C   D   E

3 Which code matches the final image? Circle the correct letter.

1 mark

MG   WG   KL   MD   WX   ?

KX ML WD MG KG

A   B   C   D   E

4 Which code matches the final image? Circle the correct letter.

1 mark

HD   HL   ML   MD   PD   ?

HD HL PL ML MD

A   B   C   D   E

Time to reflect

Mark your *Have a go* section out of 4. How are you doing so far?

Check your answers in the back of the book and see how you are doing.

Had a go
0–1 marks
Have another look at the *Worked example* on page 42. Then try these questions again.

Nearly there
2–3 marks
Look at your incorrect answers. Make sure you understand how to get the correct answer.

Nailed it!
4 marks
Congratulations! Now see whether you can get full marks on the *Timed practice*.

When you are ready, try the *Timed practice* on the next page.

Timed practice

⏱ **4**

1 Which code matches the final image? Circle the correct letter.

GK SW JM SK GW ?

SM EK GM EW FN

A B C D E

1 mark

2 Which code matches the final image? Circle the correct letter.

EU QY QS EY QB ?

QS QU EY EB ES

A B C D E

1 mark

3 Which code matches the final image? Circle the correct letter.

JF PY JF TY PF ?

TY RY BF PX BY

A B C D E

1 mark

4 Which code matches the final image? Circle the correct letter.

NA AY NY IA LY ?

NA AA LY NY IY

A B C D E

1 mark

5 Which code matches the final image? Circle the correct letter.

IN HN AN IG AG ?

AN IN AG HN HG

A B C D E

1 mark

Time to reflect

Mark your *Timed practice* section out of 5. How did you do?

Check your answers in the back of the book and write your score in the progress chart.

☐ *0–3 marks*
Scan the QR code for extra practice.
Then move on to the next practice section or
try Test 14 in your Ten-Minute Tests book.

☐ *4–5 marks*
Well done!
Move on to the next practice section or try
Test 14 in your Ten-Minute Tests book.

Checkpoint 2

In this checkpoint you will practise skills from the **Linear sequences** and **Codes** topics.

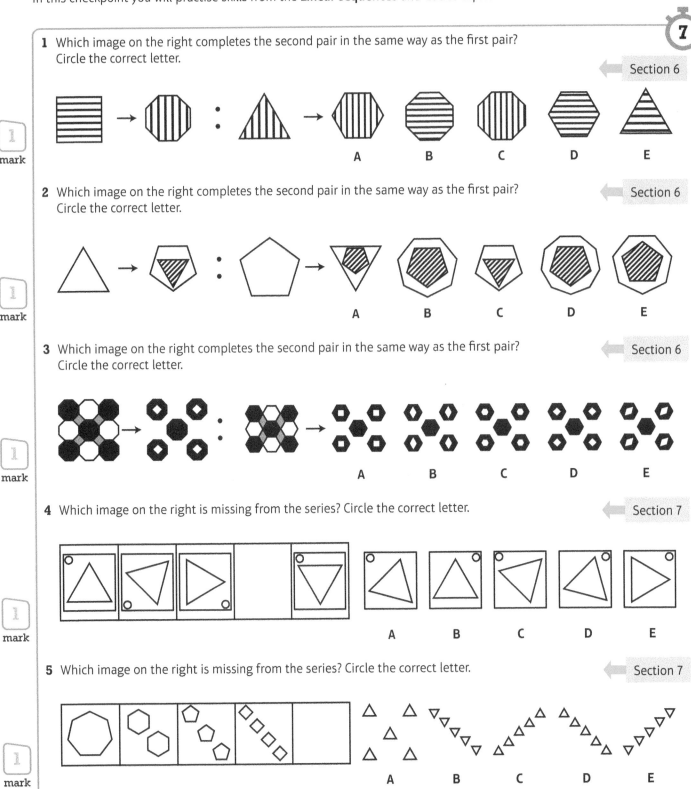

1 Which image on the right completes the second pair in the same way as the first pair? Circle the correct letter.

Section 6

1 mark

A B C D E

2 Which image on the right completes the second pair in the same way as the first pair? Circle the correct letter.

Section 6

1 mark

A B C D E

3 Which image on the right completes the second pair in the same way as the first pair? Circle the correct letter.

Section 6

1 mark

A B C D E

4 Which image on the right is missing from the series? Circle the correct letter.

Section 7

1 mark

A B C D E

5 Which image on the right is missing from the series? Circle the correct letter.

Section 7

1 mark

A B C D E

7

6 Which image on the right is missing from the series? Circle the correct letter.

Section 7

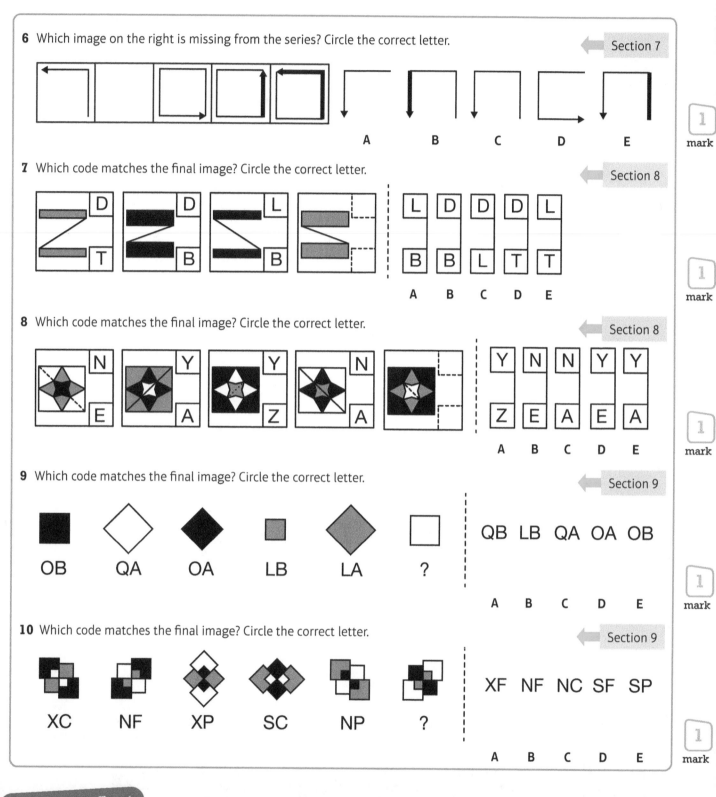

A   B   C   D   E

1 mark

7 Which code matches the final image? Circle the correct letter.

Section 8

A   B   C   D   E

1 mark

8 Which code matches the final image? Circle the correct letter.

Section 8

A   B   C   D   E

1 mark

9 Which code matches the final image? Circle the correct letter.

Section 9

OB   QA   OA   LB   LA   ?

QB LB QA OA OB

A   B   C   D   E

1 mark

10 Which code matches the final image? Circle the correct letter.

Section 9

XC   NF   XP   SC   NP   ?

XF NF NC SF SP

A   B   C   D   E

1 mark

Time to reflect

Mark your *Checkpoint* out of 10. How did you do?

1 Check your answers in the back of the book and write your score in the progress chart. If any of your answers are incorrect, use the section links to find out which practice sections to look at again.

2 Scan the QR code for extra practice.

3 Move on to the next practice section.

10 Parts of nets

Nets are 2D shapes that you can fold up to make 3D solids. In each of these questions, decide which cube on the right can be made by folding up the net on the left. Only three patterns are shown on each net.

Worked example

1 Which cube can be made from the net on the left? Circle the correct letter.

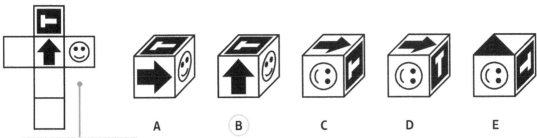

A   B   C   D   E

Imagine folding the net into a cube.

1 Look at where each face is on the net. The arrow points to the T shape. A must be wrong, because the arrow points to the smiley face.

2 Look a bit closer. The arrow points to the left-hand side of the T shape. This means C and D must also be wrong.

3 The triangle pattern in image E isn't on the net, so the answer can't be E.

Guided questions

1 Which cube can be made from the net on the left? Circle the correct letter.

> The cube might be rotated after being folded up. Any face can be at the front.

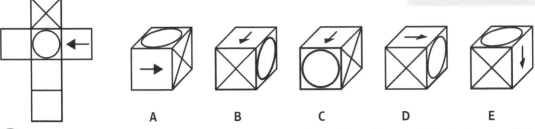

A   B   C   D   E

1 Look for shapes that point in a particular direction. The circle and cross will look the same if they are rotated, but the arrow should always point to the circle. You can cross out A, B and E because the arrow doesn't point to the circle.

2 Compare C and D. Work out which face the cross will be on if the circle is at the front. Work out which face the circle will be on if the cross is at the front. You could rotate the net to help you.

2 Which cube can be made from the net on the left? Circle the correct letter.

> Use your knowledge of orientation and rotation to answer this question.

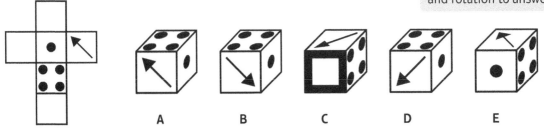

A   B   C   D   E

The arrow on the net points to a corner of the face with one dot. Use this information to cross out the wrong answers.

Guided questions

1 Which cube can be made from the net on the left? Circle the correct letter.

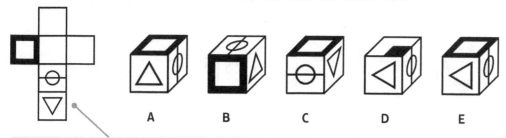

A   B   C   D   E

> If the corners of two faces on a net touch each other, those faces will share an edge on the cube. So the face with a square will touch the face with a circle.

> The circle has a straight line through it. Decide whether or not the straight line will point towards the square.

2 Which cube can be made from the net on the left? Circle the correct letter.

> Use the direction the triangle points to help you.

 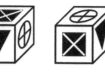

A   B   C   D   E

Have a go

1 Which cube can be made from the net on the left? Circle the correct letter.

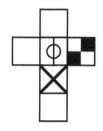   

A   B   C   D   E

> 1 mark

2 Which cube can be made from the net on the left? Circle the correct letter.

> Think about where the shapes point and how this might change when the net is folded.

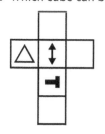

A   B   C   D   E

> 1 mark

Beyond the exam

On a normal six-sided dice, the dots on opposite faces always add up to 7. Use a ruler to draw the net of a cube or cut out one of the nets on page 97. Look at a dice and draw its dots onto the correct faces of the net. If you are confident, try to make each pattern match your dice exactly, so that each line of dots points in the right direction. Then fold your net up to check it works.

Have a go

1 Which cube can be made from the net on the left? Circle the correct letter.

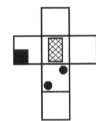

A   B   C   D   E

1 mark

> Cross off cubes that show patterns that aren't on the net.

2 Which cube can be made from the net on the left? Circle the correct letter.

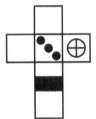

A   B   C   D   E

1 mark

> Pick two of the net's faces and decide which sides of those faces will touch each other. Use this to start crossing off wrong answers.

3 Which cube can be made from the net on the left? Circle the correct letter.

A   B   C   D   E

1 mark

> If you find one face more confusing than the others, use the easy patterns first to cross off as many wrong answers as you can.

4 Which cube can be made from the net on the left? Circle the correct letter.

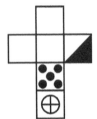

A   B   C   D   E

1 mark

Time to reflect

Mark your *Have a go* section out of 4. How are you doing so far?

Check your answers in the back of the book and see how you are doing.

☐ **Had a go**
0–1 marks

Have another look at the *Worked example* on page 48. Then try these questions again.

☐ **Nearly there**
2–3 marks

Look at your incorrect answers. Make sure you understand how to get the correct answer.

☐ **Nailed it!**
4 marks

Congratulations! Now see whether you can get full marks on the *Timed practice*.

When you are ready, try the *Timed practice* on the next page.

Timed practice

1 Which cube can be made from the net on the left? Circle the correct letter.

           A   B   C   D   E

1 mark

2 Which cube can be made from the net on the left? Circle the correct letter.

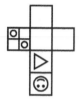

           A   B   C   D   E

1 mark

3 Which cube can be made from the net on the left? Circle the correct letter.

           A   B   C   D   E

1 mark

4 Which cube can be made from the net on the left? Circle the correct letter.

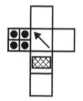

           A   B   C   D   E

1 mark

5 Which cube can be made from the net on the left? Circle the correct letter.

           A   B   C   D   E

1 mark

Time to reflect

Mark your *Timed practice* section out of 5. How did you do?

Check your answers in the back of the book and write your score in the progress chart.

☐ **0–3 marks**
Scan the QR code for extra practice.
Then move on to the next practice section or
try Test 16 in your Ten-Minute Tests book.

☐ **4–5 marks**
Well done!
Move on to the next practice section or try
Test 16 in your Ten-Minute Tests book.

11 Which cube does the net make?

In each of these questions, find which cube on the right can be made by folding up the net on the left.

Worked example

1 Which cube can be made from the net on the left? Circle the correct letter.

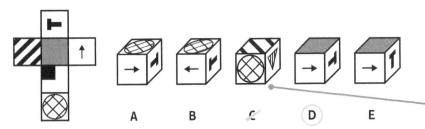

A   B   C   D   E

> All six faces of the cube are given on the net. You must imagine which faces on the net will be next to each other if the net is folded up. You might also need to decide which way up each shape will be.

> This triangle isn't on the net, so C must be wrong.

1 Look at the T and the arrow. These two faces touch at a corner, so if you folded up the net they would share an edge of the cube. The arrow would point to the base of the T.

2 B and E must be wrong because the arrow doesn't point to the base of the T.

3 A and D look the same, apart from the top face. You need to decide which top face is correct.

4 On cubes A and D, the arrow points right. Imagine rotating the net so the arrow points right, and then folding it. You could turn the page around to help you. The grey square would be on top, which means that D is the correct answer.

Guided questions

1 Which cube can be made from the net on the left? Circle the correct letter.

> These dotted faces aren't on the net, so they must be wrong.

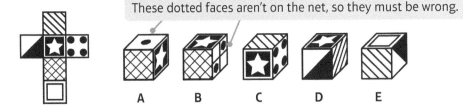

A   B   C   D   E

1 On the net, the face with a star is in the middle, so you can see clearly how it touches four of the other faces. Use the star to work out the correct answer.

2 The star should share an edge with the black half of the black and white face, so D must be wrong.

3 Look at the other faces next to the star to decide if the answer is C or E.

2 Which cube can be made from the net on the left? Circle the correct letter.

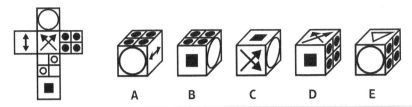

A   B   C   D   E

> Faces that are two squares apart in a straight line on the net will be opposite each other on the cube. For example, the crossed arrows must be opposite the black square. Use this information to cross out three wrong answers.

Beyond the exam

Cuboids also have six faces that connect together in the way shown by the cube nets. Find an empty cereal box and carefully take it apart so you can see the net. Look at how the sides fold together to make the edges of the box.

Guided questions

1 Which cube can be made from the net on the left? Circle the correct letter.

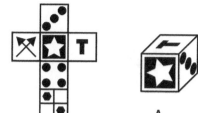 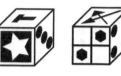

A   B   C   D   E

1 Look at the front face of each cube. Imagine folding the net around this face. You can rotate the net to help you.

2 Look at A. The star is the front face and the T is the top face. This means the net has been rotated 90° anticlockwise. So, the face on the right should be the four dots. A must be wrong.

3 Do this for each of the cubes until you find the correct answer.

2 Which cube can be made from the net on the left? Circle the correct letter.

Find patterns that look different when rotated. Use the arrow face to help you here.

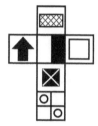

A   B   C   D   E

1 When the net is folded, the arrow will point away from the black square. Use this to decide whether A could be correct.

2 Use the net to decide which shape the arrow will point towards. Use this to work out whether B could be correct.

3 Look closely at the arrow in relation to the other faces on the net. You can use this to cross out all the wrong answers.

Have a go

1 Which cube can be made from the net on the left? Circle the correct letter.

Start by crossing out any cubes that have shapes that don't appear on the net.

A   B   C   D   E

1 mark

2 Which cube can be made from the net on the left? Circle the correct letter.

You could start by looking at the square in the middle of the net and seeing which four faces touch it.

A   B   C   D   E

1 mark

Have a go

1 Which cube can be made from the net on the left? Circle the correct letter.

     A   B   C   D   E

1 mark

2 Which cube can be made from the net on the left? Circle the correct letter.

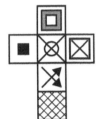

     A   B   C   D   E

1 mark

> Look for opposite faces on the net. They are not next to each other, so they can't both be visible.

3 Which cube can be made from the net on the left? Circle the correct letter.

     A   B   C   D   E

1 mark

> Look for shapes that point to each other.

4 Which cube can be made from the net on the left? Circle the correct letter.

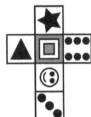

     A   B   C   D   E

1 mark

Time to reflect

Mark your *Have a go* section out of 4. How are you doing so far?

Check your answers in the back of the book and see how you are doing.

☐ **Had a go**
0–1 marks
Have another look at the *Worked example* on page 52. Then try these questions again.

☐ **Nearly there**
2–3 marks
Look at your incorrect answers. Make sure you understand how to get the correct answer.

☐ **Nailed it!**
4 marks
Congratulations! Now see whether you can get full marks on the *Timed practice*.

When you are ready, try the *Timed practice* on the next page.

Timed practice

4

1 Which cube can be made from the net on the left? Circle the correct letter.

A   B   C   D   E

1 mark

2 Which cube can be made from the net on the left? Circle the correct letter.

A   B   C   D   E

1 mark

3 Which cube can be made from the net on the left? Circle the correct letter.

A   B   C   D   E

1 mark

4 Which cube can be made from the net on the left? Circle the correct letter.

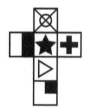

A   B   C   D   E

1 mark

5 Which cube can be made from the net on the left? Circle the correct letter.

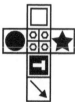

A   B   C   D   E

1 mark

Time to reflect

Mark your *Timed practice* section out of 5. How did you do?

Check your answers in the back of the book and write your score in the progress chart.

 0–3 marks
Scan the QR code for extra practice.
Then move on to the next practice section or
try Test 17 in your Ten-Minute Tests book.

4–5 marks
Well done!
Move on to the next practice section or try
Test 17 in your Ten-Minute Tests book.

Checkpoint 3

In this checkpoint you will practise skills from the **Nets** topic.

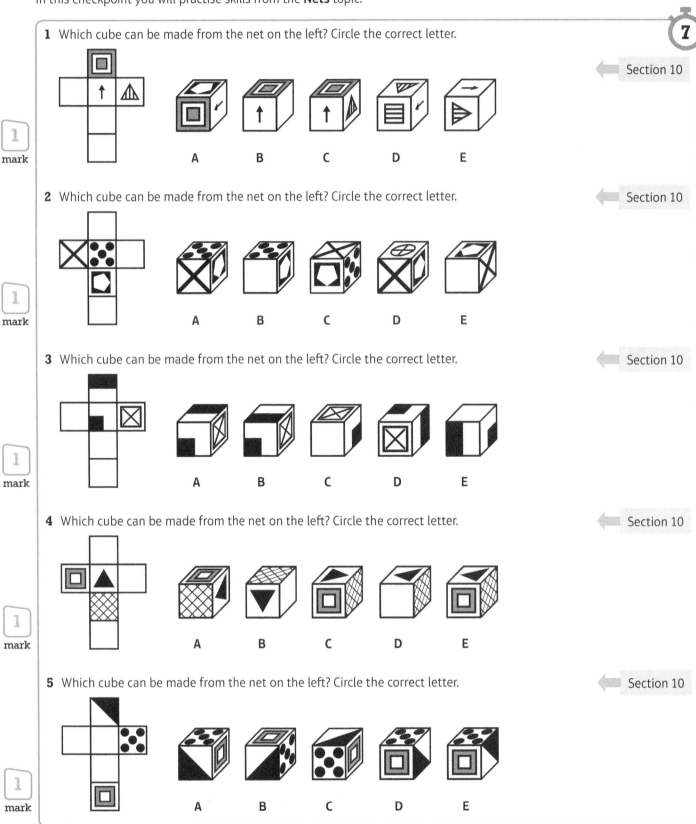

1 Which cube can be made from the net on the left? Circle the correct letter.

1 mark

Section 10

A   B   C   D   E

2 Which cube can be made from the net on the left? Circle the correct letter.

1 mark

Section 10

A   B   C   D   E

3 Which cube can be made from the net on the left? Circle the correct letter.

1 mark

Section 10

A   B   C   D   E

4 Which cube can be made from the net on the left? Circle the correct letter.

1 mark

Section 10

A   B   C   D   E

5 Which cube can be made from the net on the left? Circle the correct letter.

1 mark

Section 10

A   B   C   D   E

6 Which cube can be made from the net on the left? Circle the correct letter.

Section 11

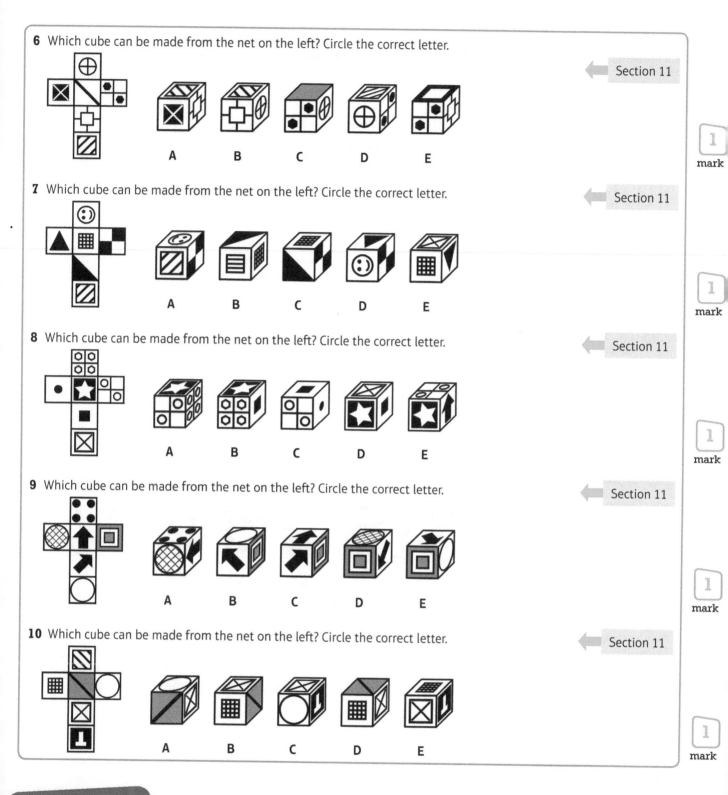

A   B   C   D   E

1 mark

7 Which cube can be made from the net on the left? Circle the correct letter.

Section 11

A   B   C   D   E

1 mark

8 Which cube can be made from the net on the left? Circle the correct letter.

Section 11

A   B   C   D   E

1 mark

9 Which cube can be made from the net on the left? Circle the correct letter.

Section 11

A   B   C   D   E

1 mark

10 Which cube can be made from the net on the left? Circle the correct letter.

Section 11

A   B   C   D   E

1 mark

Time to reflect

Mark your *Checkpoint* out of 10. How did you do?

1 Check your answers in the back of the book and write your score in the progress chart. If any of your answers are incorrect, use the section links to find out which practice sections to look at again.

2 Scan the QR code for extra practice.

3 Move on to the next practice section.

12 Cube views

In each of these questions, the same cube is shown from different angles. One of the angles shows a blank face. Use the other views of the cube to work out which image on the right should replace the blank face.

Worked examples

1 Which image on the right should replace the blank cube face? Circle the correct letter.

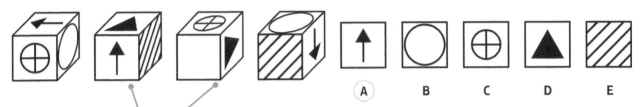

A   B   C   D   E

First, look for a pattern that you can see on both the cube with a blank face and on one of the others. Here, you can use the triangle.

You are looking at four views of the same cube. The third cube view has a blank face. You need to decide which image should go on the blank face.

1 The triangle and the circle with a cross are already shown on the cube with the blank face. They can't be on the blank face too.

2 The third cube has the triangle at the right. Imagine rotating the second cube so the triangle moves from the top to the right. The front face will still show the arrow.

3 The arrow on the second cube points to the bottom of the triangle. The bottom of the triangle is next to the blank face of the third cube. So the blank face should have the arrow on it.

2 Which image on the right should replace the blank cube face? Circle the correct letter.

Try to work these questions out quickly by rotating the cubes in your head. Lots of people find this difficult, so practise by finding matching patterns.

A   B   C   D   E

1 The blank face is next to the face with a rectangle. It is next to a long side of the rectangle, not a short side.

2 One long side of the rectangle is next to the face with a cross. So the answer might be E.

3 The other long side of the rectangle is next to the face with dots. So the answer might be C.

One of these patterns is the correct answer. Imagine drawing the cross on the blank face. The first cube would have all the same patterns as the third cube, but they would be in the wrong places. E must be wrong. This means C must be correct.

Beyond the exam

Place a normal six-sided dice on the table so you can see three faces. What is the sum of the three numbers you can see? By rotating the dice, see how many different totals you can make.

Guided questions

1 Which image on the right should replace the blank cube face? Circle the correct letter.

~~A~~   ~~B~~   C   D   E

> Cross out the patterns you can already see on the first cube.

① The cube with the blank face is the only one that doesn't have black and white squares on top. Imagine rotating it so that the squares are on top and the blank face stays at the front.

② Use the other cubes to work out which pattern will now be on the right. Cross it out.

③ Then decide which of the other two patterns is the correct answer.

2 Which image on the right should replace the blank cube face? Circle the correct letter.

A   B   C   D   E

① Look for cubes where one face is in the same position. The diagonal arrow is on the top of two of the cubes, but it has been rotated.

② Look at the two patterns the arrow is pointing to.

③ Use this information to work out the blank face. Imagine rotating the first cube.

> The blank face doesn't have to be at the front. It is on the side in this question, but you can approach it in the same way.

3 Which image on the right should replace the blank cube face? Circle the correct letter.

~~A~~   ~~B~~   ~~C~~   D   E

The first two cubes have the same top face. It has been rotated 180°. This means that the half-filled circle and the dotted circle must be on opposite faces. So, A, B and C must all be wrong.

This pattern looks the same when you rotate it 180° but different when you rotate it 90°. Try turning the page to help you.

Compare the position of D and E on the other cubes to find the correct answer.

Have a go

1 Which image on the right should replace the blank cube face? Circle the correct letter.

A   B   C   D   E

> Start by crossing out the patterns that already appear on the cube.

1 mark

Have a go

1 Which image on the right should replace the blank cube face? Circle the correct letter.

   A   B   C   D   E

> Look for a pattern that only points in one direction. If it is next to the blank face, it might show you the answer.

1 mark

2 Which image on the right should replace the blank cube face? Circle the correct letter.

   A   B   C   D   E

> Look for cubes that have two patterns in common.

1 mark

3 Which image on the right should replace the blank cube face? Circle the correct letter.

   A   B   C   D   E

> If a pattern is on all of the cubes, look at how it relates to the other images.

1 mark

4 Which image on the right should replace the blank cube face? Circle the correct letter.

   A   B   C   D   E

1 mark

5 Which image on the right should replace the blank cube face? Circle the correct letter.

   A   B   C   D   E

> Use the nets on page 97 to help you picture more challenging cubes. Look at one cube at a time and draw the faces onto the net.

1 mark

Time to reflect

Mark your *Have a go* section out of 5. How are you doing so far?

Check your answers in the back of the book and see how you are doing.

Had a go	**Nearly there**	**Nailed it!**
0–2 marks	*3–4 marks*	*5 marks*
Have another look at the *Worked example* on page 58. Then try these questions again.	Look at your incorrect answers. Make sure you understand how to get the correct answer.	Congratulations! Now see whether you can get full marks on the *Timed practice*.

When you are ready, try the *Timed practice* on the next page.

4

1 Which image on the right should replace the blank cube face? Circle the correct letter.

                                    A   B   C   D   E

1 mark

2 Which image on the right should replace the blank cube face? Circle the correct letter.

                                    A   B   C   D   E

1 mark

3 Which image on the right should replace the blank cube face? Circle the correct letter.

                                 A   B   C   D   E

1 mark

4 Which image on the right should replace the blank cube face? Circle the correct letter.

                                 A   B   C   D   E

1 mark

5 Which image on the right should replace the blank cube face? Circle the correct letter.

                                 A   B   C   D   E

1 mark

Time to reflect

Mark your *Timed practice* section out of 5. How did you do?

Check your answers in the back of the book and write your score in the progress chart.

☐ **0–3 marks**
Scan the QR code for extra practice.
Then move on to the next practice section or
try Test 21 in your Ten-Minute Tests book.

☐ **4–5 marks**
Well done!
Move on to the next practice section or try
Test 21 in your Ten-Minute Tests book.

13 2D views of 3D solids

In each of these questions, the image on the left is a 3D solid made up of cubes. Decide which 2D shape on the right it would look like if viewed from above.

Worked example

1 Which image on the right is a top-down view of the 3D solid on the left? Circle the correct letter.

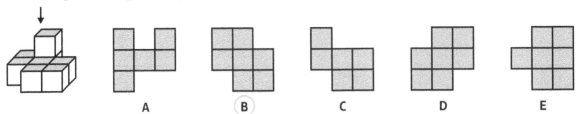

A   B   C   D   E

1 Look at the 3D solid. In the row that is closest to you, there are two cubes. They are both on the right.

2 Look at the middle row. There are three cubes.

3 Look at the row of cubes furthest away from you. There are two cubes on the left.

4 Work out which 2D image has the correct number and position of squares in each row. A only shows one square in the front row. D shows two squares, but they are on the left. These must be wrong.

5 C only has one square in the top row, and E has two but they are on the right. You can cross these out. So B is the correct answer.

> Imagine looking straight down at the 3D solid. From above, each cube looks like a square. A stack of two cubes looks the same as one cube. The row of cubes furthest from you in the 3D solid will be the top row of the top-down view.

Guided questions

1 Which image on the right is a top-down view of the 3D solid on the left? Circle the correct letter.

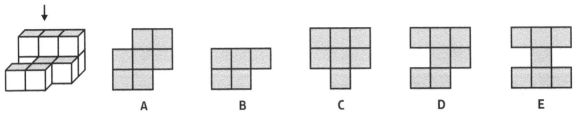

A   B   C   D   E

1 If you look closely, you can see that the middle row only has two cubes.

2 A, B and C have three squares in the middle row, so they must be wrong.

3 Count the cubes in the front and back row to decide whether the answer is D or E.

> Focus on the bottom layer of cubes in the 3D solid. If there is nothing in the top layer or the bottom layer, there will be an empty space in the top-down view.

2 Which image on the right is a top-down view of the 3D solid on the left? Circle the correct letter.

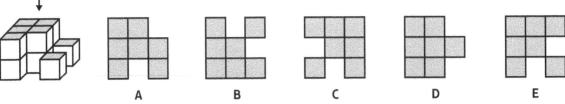

A   B   C   D   E

1 Look at each row in turn. The row closest to you has two cubes with an empty space in between them. So, you can cross out B and D.

2 Look at the row furthest from you. There are three cubes. A only has two squares, so it must be wrong.

3 Look at the middle row to work out the correct answer.

Guided questions

1 Which image on the right is a top-down view of the 3D solid on the left? Circle the correct letter.

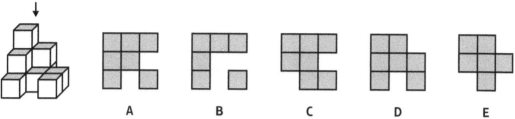

A   B   C   D   E

① Some of the cubes on the bottom layer will be hidden by cubes on top of them. So, count the highest cube on each layer. You could tick them off so you don't count any twice.

Count the cubes in the bottom layer of each row. No matter how many cubes are stacked up, they will look like one square in the top-down view.

② You are looking for top-down view made up of seven squares. B and E only have six squares. Cross them out.

③ Look for gaps in the front and back rows to work out the correct answer.

There is a gap in the middle of the furthest row. So, you are looking for top-down view with two squares in the top row. Cross out A.

2 Which image on the right is a top-down view of the 3D solid on the left? Circle the correct letter.

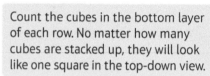
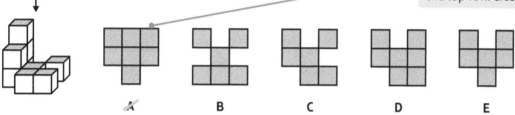

A   B   C   D   E

Have a go

1 Which image on the right is a top-down view of the 3D solid on the left? Circle the correct letter.

Check the position of the cubes in each row as well as the number.

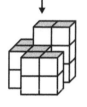

A   B   C   D   E

1 mark

2 Which image on the right is a top-down view of the 3D solid on the left? Circle the correct letter.

In images with more cubes, count how many gaps or cubes are next to one another to speed up your working out.

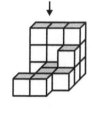 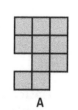 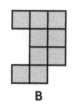 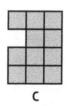 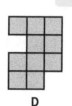 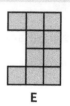

A   B   C   D   E

1 mark

Beyond the exam

A picture of something viewed directly from above is called a plan. Try drawing a plan of your room, showing all the furniture.

Have a go

1 Which image on the right is a top-down view of the 3D solid on the left? Circle the correct letter.

> Use the number of cubes next to a gap to work out how big the gap is.

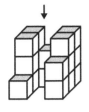

A   B   C   D   E

1 mark

2 Which image on the right is a top-down view of the 3D solid on the left? Circle the correct letter.

> Count the cubes in each row, starting with the row in front.

 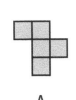

A   B   C   D   E

1 mark

3 Which image on the right is a top-down view of the 3D solid on the left? Circle the correct letter.

> For more complex shapes, you could write down the number of cubes in each row to help you.

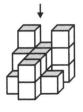 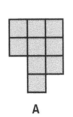 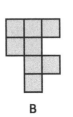 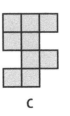  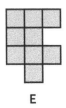

A   B   C   D   E

1 mark

4 Which image on the right is a top-down view of the 3D solid on the left? Circle the correct letter.

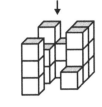 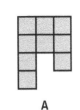 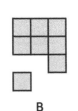 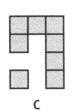 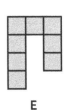

A   B   C   D   E

1 mark

Time to reflect

Mark your *Have a go* section out of 4. How are you doing so far?

Check your answers in the back of the book and see how you are doing.

	Had a go *0–1 marks*		**Nearly there** *2–3 marks*		**Nailed it!** *4 marks*

Have another look at the *Worked example* on page 62. Then try these questions again.

Look at your incorrect answers. Make sure you understand how to get the correct answer.

Congratulations! Now see whether you can get full marks on the *Timed practice*.

When you are ready, try the *Timed practice* on the next page.

Timed practice

4

1 Which image on the right is a top-down view of the 3D solid on the left? Circle the correct letter.

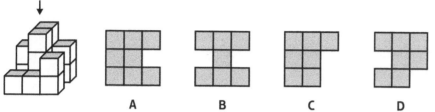

A   B   C   D   E

1 mark

2 Which image on the right is a top-down view of the 3D solid on the left? Circle the correct letter.

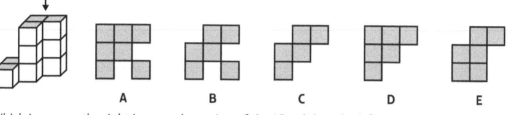

A   B   C   D   E

1 mark

3 Which image on the right is a top-down view of the 3D solid on the left? Circle the correct letter.

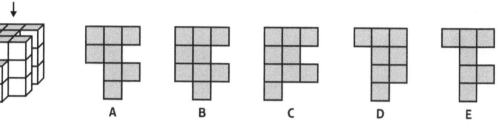

A   B   C   D   E

1 mark

4 Which image on the right is a top-down view of the 3D solid on the left? Circle the correct letter.

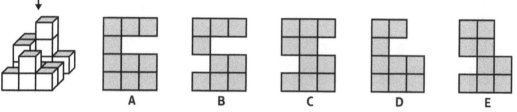

A   B   C   D   E

1 mark

5 Which image on the right is a top-down view of the 3D solid on the left? Circle the correct letter.

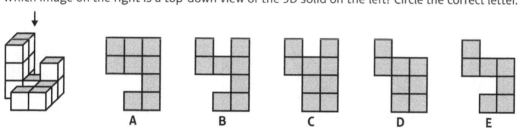

A   B   C   D   E

1 mark

Time to reflect

Mark your *Timed practice* section out of 5. How did you do?

Check your answers in the back of the book and write your score in the progress chart.

☐ *0–3 marks*
Scan the QR code for extra practice.
Then move on to the next practice section or try Test 22 in your Ten-Minute Tests book.

☐ *4–5 marks*
Well done!
Move on to the next practice section or try Test 22 in your Ten-Minute Tests book.

14 Fold along the line

In each of these questions, work out what the image on the left would look like if it were folded along the dotted line. Imagine the images are drawn on tracing paper, so that you can see both halves when the image is folded.

Worked example

1 Which image on the right shows the image on the left when folded along the dotted line? Circle the correct letter.

A   (B)   C   D   E

The right-hand side folds on top of the left-hand side. The answer will still have the same lines on the left-hand side. It will also have a reflection of the right-hand side.

The circle is symmetrical. When folded down the middle, the right-hand side will line up exactly with the left-hand side. No new curved lines will be made.

The top half of the diagonal line on the right-hand side of the image will be reflected. The line will go from the bottom left corner to the centre and then out again to the top left. The answer is B.

Guided questions

1 Which image on the right shows the image on the left when folded along the dotted line? Circle the correct letter.

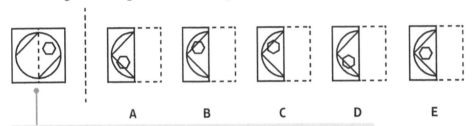

A   B   C   D   E

Look closely at the hexagon and work out how it will be reflected.

① The hexagon will be reflected on the left-hand side. It won't move up or down, so you can cross out A, D and E.
② The hexagon won't rotate either. Use this information to work out the correct answer.

2 Which image on the right shows the image on the left when folded along the dotted line? Circle the correct letter.

A   B   C   D   E

In this question, the fold line is horizontal. Half of a hexagon and a diagonal line will be reflected up.

① The hexagon is folded along a line of symmetry, so it won't add any lines to the top half of the image.
② The diagonal line will be reflected in the top-left corner of the image. You can cross out B, C and D.
③ Focus on the diagonal lines in the top half of the hexagon to decide whether the answer is A or E.

Beyond the exam

Draw a simple picture on a piece of paper. Fold it in half and imagine what the new image will look like. Now hold it up to the light. Is the new image what you thought it would look like?

Guided questions

1 Which image on the right shows the image on the left when folded along the dotted line? Circle the correct letter.

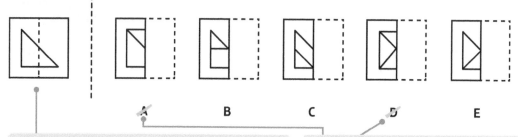

A   B   C   D   E

The section of the triangle on the right-hand side has two lines. Think carefully about how they will be reflected.

The left-hand side of the image will stay the same. The reflected lines are at the bottom of the triangle, so the top of the triangle won't change. You can cross out A and D.

2 Which image on the right shows the image on the left when folded along the dotted line? Circle the correct letter.

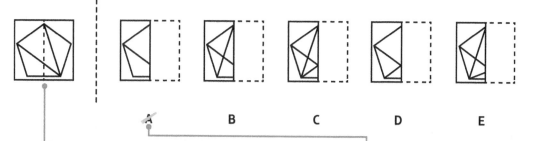

A   B   C   D   E

Look at complex images one line at a time. The pentagon is folded along a line of symmetry, so only the diagonal lines inside will change.

The pattern inside the pentagon has two diagonal lines and they aren't folded along a line of symmetry. There must be at least two diagonal lines inside the reflected image. Cross out A.

Have a go

1 Which image on the right shows the image on the left when folded along the dotted line? Circle the correct letter.

A   B   C   D   E

Try drawing the reflection and then compare your image to the possible answers.

1 mark

2 Which image on the right shows the image on the left when folded along the dotted line? Circle the correct letter.

A   B   C   D   E

The reflected image will be the same size and shape as the original image. Cross out any answers that are obviously different.

1 mark

Have a go

1 Which image on the right shows the image on the left when folded along the dotted line? Circle the correct letter.

     A   B   C   D   E

When shapes don't fold along a line of symmetry, both sides of the shape will be visible in the folded picture.

1 mark

2 Which image on the right shows the image on the left when folded along the dotted line? Circle the correct letter.

     A   B   C   D   E

Pay close attention to distances between shapes and the fold line.

1 mark

3 Which image on the right shows the image on the left when folded along the dotted line? Circle the correct letter.

     A   B   C   D   E

Break complex images down into smaller shapes and work out what their reflection would look like.

1 mark

4 Which image on the right shows the image on the left when folded along the dotted line? Circle the correct letter.

     A   B   C   D   E

Remember that the half of the image that isn't reflected won't change. Look for options that you can tell are wrong by spotting differences in this half.

1 mark

Time to reflect

Mark your *Have a go* section out of 4. How are you doing so far?

Check your answers in the back of the book and see how you are doing.

Had a go *0–1 marks*	**Nearly there** *2–3 marks*	**Nailed it!** *4 marks*
Have another look at the *Worked example* on page 66. Then try these questions again.	Look at your incorrect answers. Make sure you understand how to get the correct answer.	Congratulations! Now see whether you can get full marks on the *Timed practice*.

When you are ready, try the *Timed practice* on the next page.

Timed practice

4

1 Which image on the right shows the image on the left when folded along the dotted line? Circle the correct letter.

A   B   C   D   E

1 mark

2 Which image on the right shows the image on the left when folded along the dotted line? Circle the correct letter.

A   B   C   D   E

1 mark

3 Which image on the right shows the image on the left when folded along the dotted line? Circle the correct letter.

A   B   C   D   E

1 mark

4 Which image on the right shows the image on the left when folded along the dotted line? Circle the correct letter.

A   B   C   D   E

1 mark

5 Which image on the right shows the image on the left when folded along the dotted line? Circle the correct letter.

A   B   C   D   E

1 mark

Time to reflect

Mark your *Timed practice* section out of 5. How did you do?

Check your answers in the back of the book and write your score in the progress chart.

☐ *0–3 marks*
Scan the QR code for extra practice.
Then try the *Progress test* or try Test 27 in your Ten-Minute Tests book.

☐ *4–5 marks*
Well done!
Try the *Progress test* or try Test 27 in your Ten-Minute Tests book.

Progress test

Complete this test once you have worked through all the practice sections in this book. It covers all the topics in this book and is as hard as a real 11+ test.

1 Which image on the right is a reflection of the image on the left? Circle the correct letter.

Section 1

20

A   B   C   D   E

1 mark

2 Which image on the right is a reflection of the image on the left? Circle the correct letter.

Section 1

A   B   C   D   E

1 mark

3 Which image on the right is a rotation of the image on the left? Circle the correct letter.

Section 2

A   B   C   D   E

1 mark

4 Which image on the right is a rotation of the image on the left? Circle the correct letter.

Section 2

A   B   C   D   E

1 mark

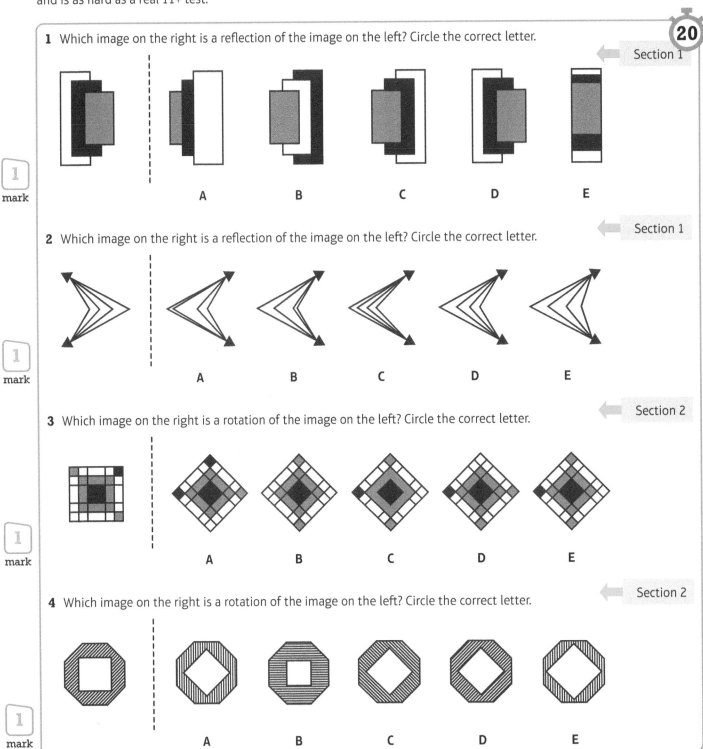

5 Which image on the right contains the image on the left? Circle the correct letter. ← Section 3

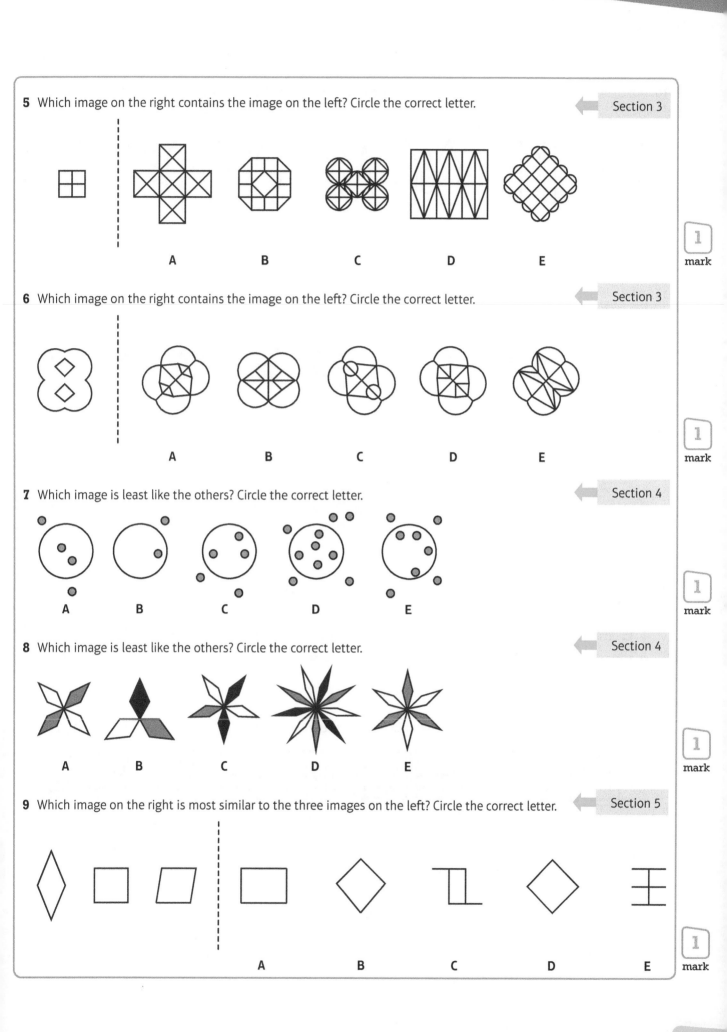

A   B   C   D   E

1 mark

6 Which image on the right contains the image on the left? Circle the correct letter. ← Section 3

A   B   C   D   E

1 mark

7 Which image is least like the others? Circle the correct letter. ← Section 4

A   B   C   D   E

1 mark

8 Which image is least like the others? Circle the correct letter. ← Section 4

A   B   C   D   E

1 mark

9 Which image on the right is most similar to the three images on the left? Circle the correct letter. ← Section 5

A   B   C   D   E

1 mark

10 Which image on the right is most similar to the two images on the left? Circle the correct letter. Section 5

11 Which image on the right completes the second pair in the same way as the first pair? Circle the correct letter. Section 6

12 Which image on the right completes the second pair in the same way as the first pair? Circle the correct letter. Section 6

13 Which image on the right is missing from the series? Circle the correct letter. Section 7

14 Which image on the right is missing from the series? Circle the correct letter. Section 7

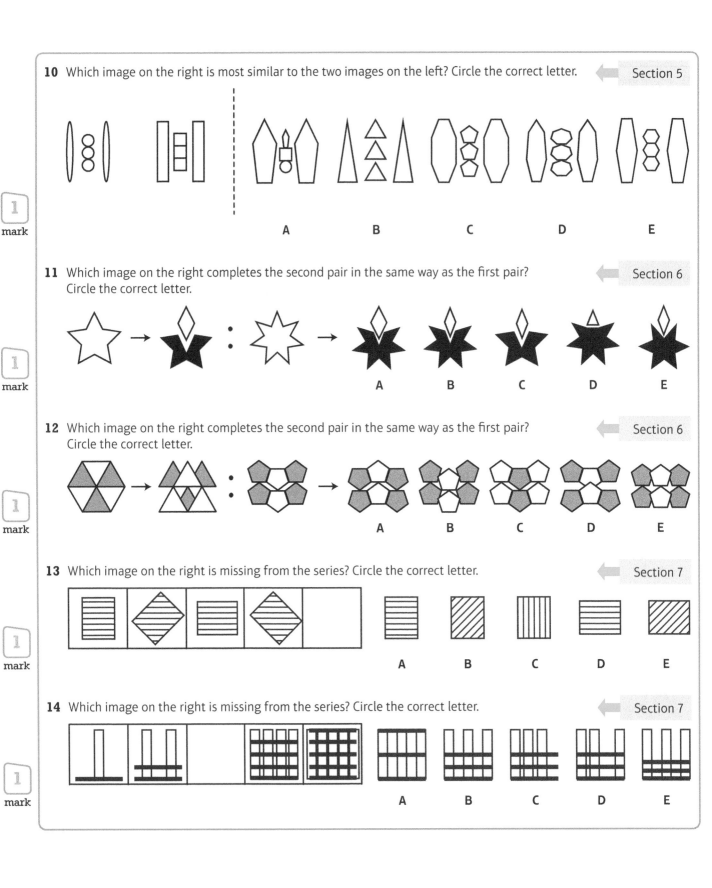

1 mark

1 mark

1 mark

1 mark

1 mark

A   B   C   D   E

15 Which code matches the final image? Circle the correct letter.
Section 8

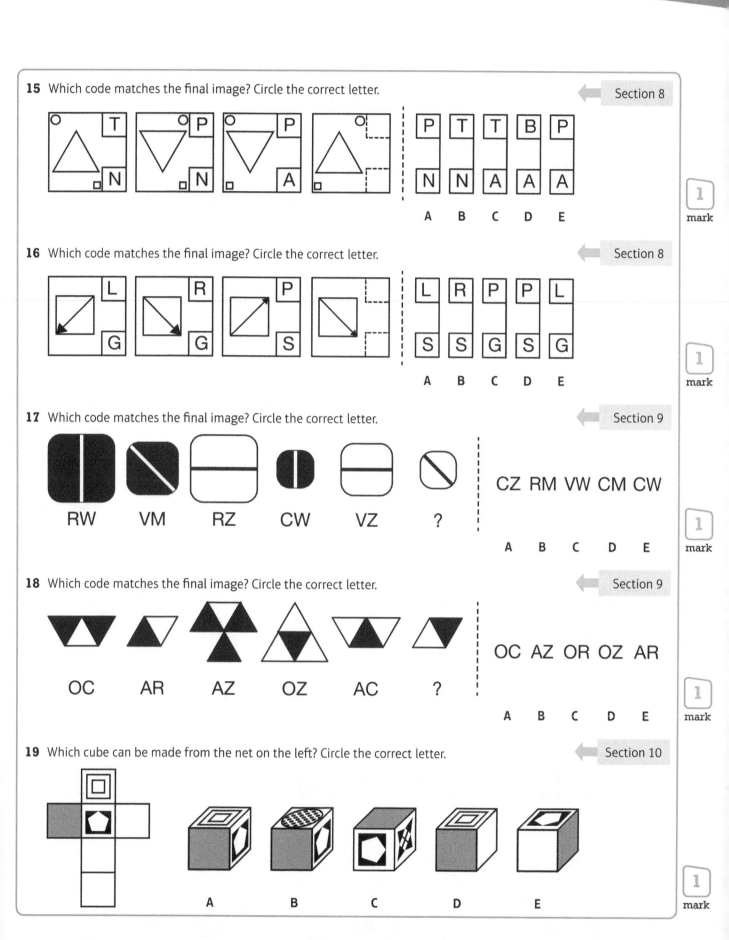

A   B   C   D   E

1 mark

16 Which code matches the final image? Circle the correct letter.
Section 8

A   B   C   D   E

1 mark

17 Which code matches the final image? Circle the correct letter.
Section 9

RW   VM   RZ   CW   VZ   ?

CZ RM VW CM CW

A   B   C   D   E

1 mark

18 Which code matches the final image? Circle the correct letter.
Section 9

OC   AR   AZ   OZ   AC   ?

OC AZ OR OZ AR

A   B   C   D   E

1 mark

19 Which cube can be made from the net on the left? Circle the correct letter.
Section 10

A   B   C   D   E

1 mark

20 Which cube can be made from the net on the left? Circle the correct letter.

Section 10

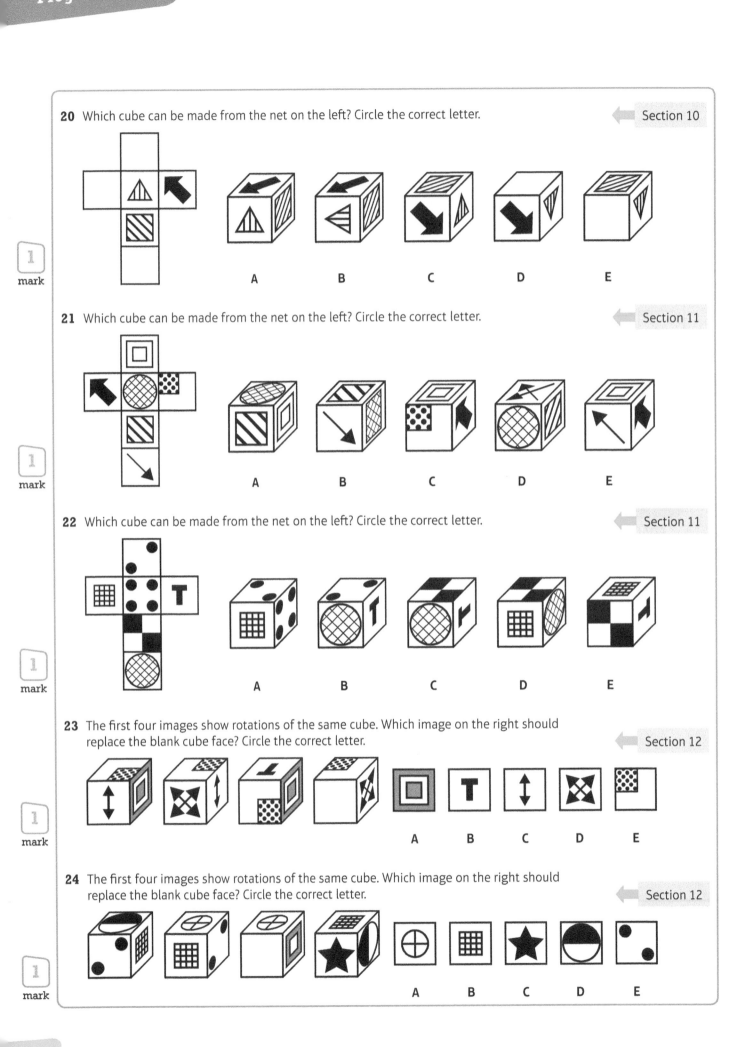

A   B   C   D   E

1 mark

21 Which cube can be made from the net on the left? Circle the correct letter.

Section 11

A   B   C   D   E

1 mark

22 Which cube can be made from the net on the left? Circle the correct letter.

Section 11

A   B   C   D   E

1 mark

23 The first four images show rotations of the same cube. Which image on the right should replace the blank cube face? Circle the correct letter.

Section 12

A   B   C   D   E

1 mark

24 The first four images show rotations of the same cube. Which image on the right should replace the blank cube face? Circle the correct letter.

Section 12

A   B   C   D   E

1 mark

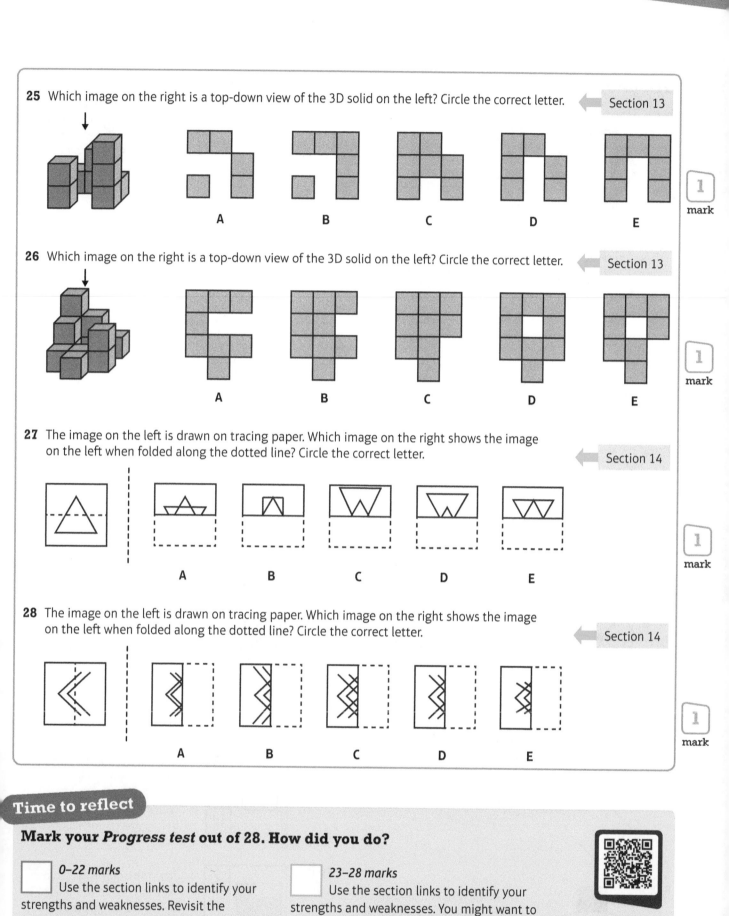

25 Which image on the right is a top-down view of the 3D solid on the left? Circle the correct letter. ← Section 13

A B C D E

1 mark

26 Which image on the right is a top-down view of the 3D solid on the left? Circle the correct letter. ← Section 13

A B C D E

1 mark

27 The image on the left is drawn on tracing paper. Which image on the right shows the image on the left when folded along the dotted line? Circle the correct letter. ← Section 14

A B C D E

1 mark

28 The image on the left is drawn on tracing paper. Which image on the right shows the image on the left when folded along the dotted line? Circle the correct letter. ← Section 14

A B C D E

1 mark

Time to reflect

Mark your *Progress test* out of 28. How did you do?

☐ *0–22 marks*
Use the section links to identify your strengths and weaknesses. Revisit the practice sections you scored the lowest in and then scan the QR code to try more mixed questions.

☐ *23–28 marks*
Use the section links to identify your strengths and weaknesses. You might want to revisit the practice sections you scored the lowest in, before moving on to Practice Book 2.

Answers

Diagnostic test

Page 2

1 A:

B has been rotated, not reflected. In C, the middle shape is at the wrong angle. In D and E, the white area is a different shape.

2 D:

A has been rotated, not reflected. B is the same as the image on the left. In C, the middle stars have swapped colours. In E, the black star is the wrong way up.

3 C:

In A and B, the colours of the squares have changed. In D and E, the triangle is the wrong shape.

4 C:

In A, the arrowheads are the same size. In B and D, the arrowheads are pointing the wrong way. In E, the line connecting the arrows is too short.

Page 3

5 A:

In B, the triangles are too big. In C, they are not triangles. In D and E, the triangles are the wrong size.

6 E:

In A, B and D, the two stars aren't joined in one continuous shape. In C, two of the points are too short.

7 E:

All the other squares have the same orientation.

8 D:

In all the other images, the black shape is in front of the white shape.

9 E:

The images on the left each contain three shapes, which are identical apart from their size. The smaller shapes are centred inside the bigger ones.

Page 4

10 B:

B is the only image that is the same size as the images on the left.

11 C:

The outer shape flips vertically and the two shapes swap colours.

12 A: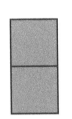

The image splits into two identical shapes that sit one on top of the other. The dotted fill becomes a grey fill.

13 B:

The arrow and line alternate between top and bottom. The triangle rotates clockwise.

14 C:

The rectangle becomes increasingly rounded, and the direction of the diagonal lines alternates.

Page 5

15 A:

The top letter is the direction of the lines (R – horizontal, B – vertical). The bottom letter is the size of the square (W – large, N – small).

16 B: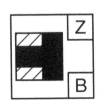

The top letter is the colour of the T shape (Z – black, T – white, D – grey). The bottom letter is the direction of the lines (W – horizontal, M – vertical, B – diagonal).

17 D:

The first letter is the shape (Y – pentagon, W – hexagon, L – heptagon). The second letter is the line style (U – dashed, N – solid).

18 A:

The first letter is the colour of the top-left circle (W – black, A – white, K – grey). The second letter is the colour of the top-right circle (S – black, I – white, Q – grey).

19 D:

A is wrong because the triangle is rotated incorrectly. B and C have patterns that are not on the net. E is wrong because the blank face should have the pentagon on it.

Page 6

20 E:

A and D are wrong because the blank faces should have patterns on them. In B, the line through the circle should be vertical, not horizontal. In C, the diagonal lines should go in the other direction.

21 C:

A and D are wrong because the white square and the grid square should be on opposite sides. B and E have patterns that are not on the net.

22 D:

A is wrong because the spotted square should be on the left-hand side. The five dots and the crossed circle are on opposite sides, so B and C are wrong. E has its top and side faces swapped.

23 A:

C and E are already on the cube. The second and fourth cubes show that B and E are on opposite sides, so B must be underneath. D is next to one of the white edges of C, so cannot be the answer.

24 A:

B is already on the cube. The fourth cube shows that E cannot be correct because it is next to the bottom of the star. Comparing the third and fourth cubes shows that C must be opposite B. By comparing the first and second cubes, you can see that D must be on the bottom of the second cube.

Page 7

25 C:

The correct answer must have two cubes on the right in the top row, three cubes in the second row and two cubes, with a gap in the middle, in the bottom row.

26 C: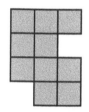

The correct answer must have three cubes in the top row, two cubes on the left in the second row, three cubes in the third row and two cubes on the right in the bottom row.

27 A:

In B, C and D, one or both of the missing segments in the circles are in the wrong place. In E, the missing segments are too big.

28 C:

In A, B and E, the folded over part of the hexagon is the wrong size. In D, the whole shape is too small.

1 Reflection

Page 8 Guided question

1 B:

In A and C, the 4 and 3 are in the wrong order, so they cannot be a reflection. In D, both numbers are upside down. In E, the 3 has not been reflected.

Page 9 Guided questions

1 A:

In B, C and E, the stars are in different positions from the image on the left. In D, the stars are upside down.

2 C:

In A, the outside circle has not been reflected. In B, the inside circle has not been reflected. In D, the colours are swapped. In E, the inside circle is at the wrong angle.

3 E:

In A, the shape is upside down. In B, the shape has not been reflected. In C and D, the triangles are the wrong shape.

4 C:

In A and E, the inside shape has not been reflected. In B, the outside shape has not been reflected. In D, the outside shape has been rotated.

Page 10 Have a go

1 C:

In A, B and D, the shapes are in different positions from the image on the left. In E, the pentagon has not been reflected.

2 D: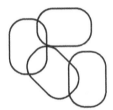

The rounded rectangles overlap differently in the other images.

3 B:

The triangles are different sizes in the other images.

4 A:

The shading of the grid squares is different in the other images.

5 D:

In A, B and C, the shapes are layered differently. In E, the kite shape has not been reflected.

Page 11 Timed practice

1 E:

In A and D, the colours of the hexagons are different from the image on the left. In B and C, the black hexagon is on top of the white one.

2 A:

In B, the bold dashed line is not reflected. In C, there are two bold dashed lines. In D, the grey triangles are in the wrong places. In E, there is no bold dashed line.

3 B:

In A, the colours in the small circle segments are wrong. In C and D, the outlines of the shapes are in the wrong places, and in E, the square is in the wrong position.

4 E:

In A, the shape has been flipped upside down. In B, C and D, some of the black and white striped sections are in the wrong positions.

5 D:

In the other images, at least one of the diagonally shaded boxes runs in the wrong direction.

2 Rotation

Page 12 Guided questions

1 D:

A is wrong because the arrowhead at the end of the longer line is too large. B has been reflected before being rotated. In C, the short arrow is the wrong way around. In E, there is an extra arrowhead.

2 C: 9D / 5C

A is wrong because the 6 and the D are swapped around. B has been reflected before being rotated. In D, the 6 is upside down. In E, the D6 is swapped with the 5C.

Page 13 Guided question

1 D:

In A, B and C, the shapes have changed position so they cannot be rotations. In E, the grey star has no black outline.

Page 13 Have a go

1 E:

In A, the arrowheads are both on the same side. In B, the shape has been reflected. In C, both arrowheads are the same size. In D, the big arrowhead points to the wrong place.

2 E:

In A and B, the small stars are the wrong way around. In C and D, the larger white star is on top of the dotted star.

3 B:

In A, one of the arrows is pointing to the wrong corner. In C and E, the arrowheads are too close together. D is a reflection.

Page 14 Have a go

1 B:

In A, the middle line is on the wrong side of the image. In C, all the lines are too thick. In D, the middle line is too long. In E, the larger diamonds are too big.

2 D:

In A, the arrows are too close together. In B, C and E, at least one arrow is pointing in the wrong direction.

3 C:

In A, the line is too long. B has been reflected before being rotated. In D, the grey heart is black. In E, the stars are too big.

4 E:

In A, the arrows are too close together. In B, there is an extra arrow. In C and D, the arrows are at the wrong angle.

Page 15 Timed practice

1 E:

In A, the arrow is at the wrong angle. In B and C, the diamonds are the wrong shape. In D, the triangle is on top of the diamonds.

2 C: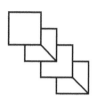

In A, some lines are curved. In B and E, some lines are in the wrong place. In D, some lines are not straight.

3 A:

In B and C the line coming from the central 'Z' shape is in the wrong place. In D, the top and bottom parts of the 'Z' are too long. E has been reflected before being rotated.

4 A:

B is wrong because it has been reflected before being rotated. In C and D, the black triangle outline is too small. In E, the white heptagon is upside down.

5 B:

In A and C, the arrows point the wrong way. In D, the larger triangle is on top of the smaller triangle. E has been reflected before being rotated.

3 Hidden shapes

Page 16 Guided questions

1 C:

In the other images, the small square is the wrong size or is a different shape.

2 B:

In the other images, the triangle is positioned differently inside the kite shape.

1 D:

In A and E, the curved line is different. In B, the straight line is on the wrong side. In C, the hidden shape has been reflected.

2 C:

A is wrong because it has been reflected. In B, the curved line is different. In D, the oval is rotated incorrectly. In E, the curved line is made of straight lines.

Page 17 Have a go

1 B:

In A and E, the triangle and rectangle overlap, and in A the triangle is also too small. C does not have a rectangle that is the right size. In D, the hidden shape has been reflected.

2 D:

In A, the spiral does not make enough turns. In B, C and E, the spiral does not touch the rounded square the correct number of times.

Page 18 Have a go

1 E:

In A, the hidden shape has been reflected. In B, the arrowhead is in the wrong place. In C and D, one of the two shorter lines is in the wrong place.

2 D:

In A, the arrow shape has been reflected. In B and C, the arrowheads are the wrong size. In E, the line connecting the end of the arrows is diagonal instead of straight.

3 A:

In B, some of the lines are curved. In C, two lines are at the wrong angle. D has rhombi rather than squares. In E, one of the lines is missing.

4 B: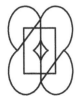

In A and C, the rectangle is the wrong size. In D, the diamond is too big. In E, the diamond is the wrong shape.

Page 19 Timed practice

1 B:

In A, the rectangle is on top of the triangle. In C and E, the rectangle touches the top corner of the triangle. In D, the rectangle is too short.

2 C:

In A, the rectangle is too small. In B, the triangle is too small. D does not have the rectangle. In E, the rectangle is positioned too high up.

3 D:

In A and C, one of the two internal lines is missing. In B and E, the lines do not join in a corner of the pentagon.

4 D:

In A, there is only one curved line. B does not have the middle straight line. In C, the curved lines are in the wrong place, and in E the curved lines are different.

5 A:

In the other images, the right angles in the hidden shape are in the wrong place. In D, the hidden shape has been reflected.

4 Odd one out

Page 20 Guided questions

1 E:

All of the other images contain one solid black arrow and one dashed black arrow. E has two solid black arrows.

2 D:

All of the other arrows point anti-clockwise.

Page 21 Guided questions

1 C:

In all of the other images, the arrow crosses over the two shapes. In C, the arrow is inside the right-hand star.

2 C:

Four of these images are exactly the same shape, but rotated. C is the only image that does not contain a joined-up rectangle.

Page 21 Have a go

1 E:

E is the only image where the triangle has been rotated.

2 A:

In all of the other images there are the same number of small shapes as points on the star. In A, the star has five points but there are six small shapes.

Page 22 Have a go

1 A:

A is the only image where the diagonal lines touch the left-hand corners of the large rectangle, rather than the right-hand corners.

2 D:

D is the only image that contains two curved lines. The other images only have one.

3 B:

B is the only image that doesn't contain a vertical line.

4 C:

In all of the other images the arrowhead points into a corner. In C, the arrowhead points into the centre of the triangle.

Page 23 Timed practice

1 C:

C is the only image in which both circles are grey.

2 E:

E is the only image in which three of the circles are the same colour.

3 B:

In all the other images there are the same number of white squares as grey squares. In B, there are seven white squares and five grey squares.

4 C:

C is the only image in which a pair of arrows is not joined at the ends.

5 D:

D is the only image in which the arrow does not make a right angle with the side of the shape. It is also the only image in which the arrow does not point to the opposite side of the shape.

5 Which image belongs?

Page 24 Guided questions

1 C:

The two images on the left are both divided into six equal parts, three of which are shaded grey. C is the only image that shares these features.

2 E:

The two images on the left both have a white shape and an identical black shape. These shapes overlap in a row, with the black shape at the back. E is the only shape that shares these features.

Page 25 Guided questions

1 D: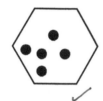

The two images on the left both have a shape that contains one less dot than it has sides. D is a hexagon with five dots inside.

2 A:

The three images on the left each contain a large square in front of a small circle, with its corner in the centre of the circle. There are two shapes in front of the large square, one of which is regular. A is the only image that shares these features.

Page 25 Have a go

1 D:

The two images on the left both have a white rectangle on the same side of the black rectangle as the star. In both, the side of the star attached to the black rectangle has two black segments and one white segment. D is the only shape that shares these features.

2 E: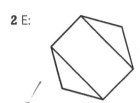

The two images on the left are symmetrical and have two parallel lines that mark off two regions that are the same size and shape. E is the only shape that shares these features.

1 C:

The two images on the left both contain exactly three lines that travel from corner to corner. C is the only shape that shares this feature. A, D and E are wrong because some of the lines travel from side to side and B is wrong because it has five lines.

2 D:

The three images on the left all have one black ring and the lines inside the image are in the same position. D is the only shape that shares these features.

3 E:

The three images on the left each contain two parallel rectangles that do not overlap, one of which contains horizontal lines. C cannot be correct, because the rectangles are smaller. E is the only image that has two parallel rectangles of the same size, one of which has horizontal lines.

4 C:

The three images on the left all contain the same three shapes, two of which are white and one of which is black. The circle and rectangle are always on opposite sides of the oval and are an equal distance from it. C is the only shape that shares these features.

1 D:

The two images on the left both have a diagonal line separating an equal number of black and white circles. Additionally, the black and white circles invert when reflected in the line. D is the only image that shares these features.

2 C:

The two images on the left both have the same type of shape in three different colours. The black shape is the biggest, and the white and striped shapes are the same size. None of the shapes overlap. C is the only shape that shares these features.

3 B:

The two images on the left each contain two rounded squares. Also, they both have an opaque, regular polygon on top of the rounded squares. B is the only shape that shares these features, as it includes a rounded square of the same size and orientation and there is a regular polygon (hexagon) on top.

4 B:

The two images on the left both have the same number of lines inside the square as circles, and contain at least one white circle and one black circle. B is the only shape that shares these features, as it has three lines and three circles (two white, one black).

5 B:

The three images on the left all have three lines with arrowheads, two of which have arrowheads the same size, and three lines without arrowheads. B is the only shape that shares these features.

Checkpoint 1

1 E:

In A, B and C, some lines are at the wrong angle. D has not been reflected.

2 C:

In A, grey triangles do not touch in the middle. In D and E, the triangles are in a different position. B has been rotated, not reflected.

3 B: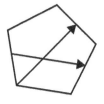

In A, C and D, the arrows are in the wrong place. In E, the image has been reflected before being rotated.

4 A:

In the other images, the inner square moves relative to the pentagon.

5 B:

A is missing one of the points of the hidden shape. In C, the shape is not complete. In D and E, the triangular gap in the hidden shape is missing.

Page 29

6 D:

In the other images, the triangle inside the hexagon is missing.

7 D:

The other arrows point to a white circle containing a black square. D is the only one that points to a white square containing a black circle.

8 C:

The other images are all rotations of the same shape. C is the only one that is a reflection.

9 D:

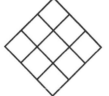

The images on the left can both be divided into nine equal squares.

10 B:

The images on the left all overlap and are the same shape and orientation.

6 Complete the pair

Page 30 Guided questions

1 D:

The colour of the largest rectangle moves to the centre, and the colours of the middle two rectangles move outwards. The largest circle in the question is shaded, so in the correct answer the centre circle must be shaded. The colours of the middle two circles move outwards, so the medium circle must be black and the outer circle must be white.

2 A:

The sides of the small shape disappear and the top and bottom of it are extended. A is the only image where the height of the horizontal lines has stayed the same.

Page 31 Guided questions

1 C:

Four extra lines appear inside the square and the lines are rotated 45° clockwise.

2 B:

The shape rotates 90° clockwise. This means the big black triangle must be at the bottom right and the small black triangle must be at the top left.

Page 31 Have a go

1 E:

The inner shape flips vertically, and the outer and inner shapes swap colours. So the circle must be grey and the two triangles must be white and flipped vertically.

2 B:

The outer shape disappears. The inner shape flips vertically, loses the line in the middle and becomes the colour of the outer shape. A looks like it could be the answer but it is too small.

Page 32 Have a go

1 D:

The shape is flipped horizontally and the arrowheads get smaller.

2 D:

The outer shape rotates 90° clockwise and becomes black, while the inner shape rotates 90° anticlockwise.

3 C:

The image rotates 90° anticlockwise, and the half of the shape opposite the black triangle is filled in black.

4 C: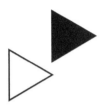

The shape is flipped vertically and reduced in size. A copy of the new shape is filled in black and placed above and to the right of the white shape.

Page 33 Timed practice

1 D:

The image rotates 90°, and the inner shape moves to the front and partly covers the black shape.

2 D:

The shape becomes smaller. A horizontally reflected copy of the shape is added to its right-hand side and overlaps with it. There is no line between the shape and its reflection.

3 D:

The shape rotates 90° anticlockwise, and all the black and white sections swap colours.

4 A:

The outline of the shape rotates 90°. The stripes do not rotate. An identical shape is attached beneath.

5 E:

The number of points on the star halves, and the number of sides on the polygon doubles. E contains a star with five points and a polygon with six sides.

7 Complete the series

Page 34 Guided questions

1 B: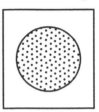

At each step, the circle increases in size and alternates between white and a dotted pattern.

2 A: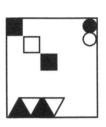

An extra square and circle are added each time, and a triangle is removed. The colours alternate.

Page 35 Guided questions

1 E:

Each cut-out segment of the circle is bigger than the previous one, and alternates between being on the left and on the right.

2 B:

At each step, the vertical line gets thinner and the square gets bigger.

Page 35 Have a go

1 B:

Each shape has one side fewer than the previous shape, and the line alternates between vertical and horizontal.

2 B: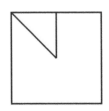

The diagonal line runs from the centre of the square to the corner and rotates clockwise. The other line runs from the centre of the square to the centre of the side and rotates anticlockwise.

Page 36 Have a go

1 D:

The black circle moves clockwise and a line is added that joins the centre of the circles.

2 D:

In the first, third and fifth steps, the number of vertical lines increases by one each time.

3 C:

Grey moves anticlockwise and black moves clockwise around the shapes.

4 A:

The cross rotates anticlockwise. The squares and circle move in one position each step, in the pattern square, square, circle. The smallest shape becomes the biggest shape in the next step.

Page 37 Timed practice

1 D: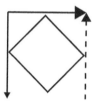

The rectangle rotates by 45°. The arrows each move in the direction shown by their arrowhead.

2 A: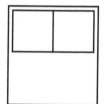

The square in the top-left corner stays in the same place. The other square moves clockwise around the picture.

3 E:

The bottom triangle is always white. The colours move clockwise around the other three triangles.

4 C:

The arrow alternates direction while the other lines take it in turns to move clockwise around the picture.

5 B:

Each image contains one circle fewer than the previous image. The arrows point to the circles that are not in the following image.

8 Codes in boxes

Page 38 Guided questions

1 D:

The top letter is the shape (A – heart, V – droplet). The bottom letter is the size (B – big, G – small).

2 B:

The top letter is the number of lines (M – one, C – two). The bottom letter is the orientation of the hexagon (P – angle at the bottom, Y – side at the bottom).

Page 39 Guided questions

1 A:

The top letter is the size of the longer arrow's head (G – big, S – small). The bottom letter is the orientation of the arrows (J – longer arrow on top, B – longer arrow on bottom).

2 C:

The top letter is the orientation of the star (T – one point at the top, O – two points at the top). The bottom letter is the colour of the star (C – crosshatched, A – black, V – white).

Page 39 Have a go

1 D:

The top letter is the presence of a hexagon (T – hexagon, A – no hexagon). The bottom letter is the colour of the circle (M – black, S – white).

2 E: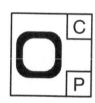

The top letter is the outer shape (C – rounded square, T – circle). The bottom letter is the inner colour (D – black, P – white).

Page 40 Have a go

1 A: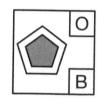

The top letter is the orientation of the pentagon (O – angle at top, L – side at the top). The bottom letter is the presence of an inner shape (K – no inner shape, B – inner shape).

2 A:

The top letter is the outer colour (Z – black, Q – white). The bottom letter is the inner colour (O – white, T – grey, R – black).

3 D:

The top letter is the colour of the outer circle (H – dotted, P – grey). The bottom letter is the orientation of the inner square (I – angles at the top and bottom, A – sides at the top and bottom).

4 B:

The top letter is the colour of the outer shape (B – dotted, P – white, R – grey). The bottom letter is the orientation (G – one point at the top and bottom, B – two points at the top and bottom).

Page 41 Timed practice

1 D:

The top letter is the orientation of the line (L – vertical, U – horizontal). The bottom letter is whether the line is dashed or solid (A – solid, V – dashed).

2 C:

The top letter is the colour of the octagon (W – white, R – black, M – grey). The bottom letter is the position of the octagon (D – at the top, T – at the bottom).

3 B:

The top letter is the presence of a diagonal line from top left to bottom right (D – line, O – no line). The bottom letter is the presence of a diagonal line from bottom left to top right (F – line, T – no line).

4 C:

The top letter is the colour of the middle shape (U – black, K – grey). The bottom letter is the orientation of the middle shape (E – angle at the top and bottom, V – side at the top and bottom).

5 D:

The top letter is the number of corners that are not touched by a line (K – two, D – four). The bottom letter is the number of sides the shape has (H – ten sides, X – eight sides, D – six sides).

9 Codes in lists

Page 42 Guided questions

1 C: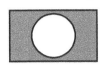

BT

The first letter is the colour of the circle (R – black, B – white, O – grey). The second letter is the colour of the rectangle (T – grey, F – black, A – white).

2 C:

OL

The first letter is the colour of the circle (I – black, Q – white, O – grey). The second letter is the number of sides the shapes have (D – three, L – five, Z – seven).

Page 43 Guided questions

1 E:

JS

The first letter is the orientation of the straight lines (Z – two lines at the top of the circle, J – one line at the top of the circle). The second letter is the thickness of the straight lines (W – thickest, S – medium thickness, K – thinnest).

2 C:

SE

The first letter is the line style (R – solid line, S – dashed line). The second letter is the direction of the arrow (U – upwards, E – downwards, P – left, K – right).

Page 43 Have a go

1 E:

OJ

The first letter is the number of objects (D – one, O – two). The second letter is the size of the pentagon (W – big, V – medium, J – small).

2 D:

RE

The first letter is the arrangement of the arrowheads (C – two arrowheads, H – only left-hand arrowhead, R – only right-hand arrowhead). The second letter is the shape of the star (A – six points, X – five points, E – seven points, U – eight points).

Page 44 Have a go

1 B:

QG

The first letter is the shape (T – small oval, M – long oval, Q – wide oval). The second letter is the colour (L – white, C – grey, G – black).

2 A:

PC

The first letter is the size of the circle (N – medium, S – small, P – big). The second letter is the direction of the arrow (V – up to the left, C – up to the right, O – down to the left, X – down to the right).

3 B:

ML

The first letter is the position of the line (M – top left to bottom, W – top left to top right, K – top right to bottom). The second letter is the position of the arrow (G – top right to bottom, L – top right to top left, D – bottom to top right).

4 B:

HL

The first letter is the smallest inside shape (P – pentagon, H – square, M – triangle). The second letter is the outside colour (D – crosshatched, L – black).

Page 45 Timed practice

1 C:

GM

The first letter is the arrangement of the arrowheads (G – pointing upwards, S – pointing downwards, J – no arrowhead). The second letter is the size of the triangle (K – small, W – big, M – medium).

2 E:

ES

The first letter is the thickness of the outline (E – thin outline, Q – thick outline). The second letter is the angle of the line shading (U – diagonal from bottom left to top right, Y – horizontal, S – diagonal from top left to bottom right, B – vertical).

3 A:

TY

The first letter is the angle of the line through the shape (J – 60° from horizontal, P – 90°, T – 30°). The second letter is the style of the line (F – white, Y – black).

4 A:

NA

The first letter is the number of white regions (N – one, A – two, I – zero, L – three). The second letter is the number of lines or regions (A – one line, two regions, Y – two lines, four regions).

5 D:

HN

The first letter is the thickness of the horizontal line (I – medium, H – thin, A – thick). The second letter is the number of vertical lines on top of the horizontal line (N – two, G – one).

Checkpoint 2

Page 46

1 D:

The stripes rotate by 90° and the number of sides the shape has doubles.

2 B:

The shape shrinks, is reflected and becomes striped. A larger shape with two extra sides appears around it.

3 B:

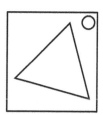

The white shapes disappear. The grey shapes change to white and move inside the black shapes at the same size and orientation.

4 D:

The circle moves anticlockwise around the corners. The triangle rotates clockwise 45°.

5 D:

The number of shapes increases by one and the number of sides on each shape decreases by one. The shapes alternate between having a corner and a side at the bottom. They are organised in a diagonal line, going down left to right.

Page 47

6 C:

The arrow moves anticlockwise around one side of a square. The line is thicker where it overlaps.

7 E:

The top letter is the direction of the diagonal line (D – upwards from left to right, L – downwards from left to right). The bottom letter is the colour of the rectangles (B – black, T – grey).

8 B:

The top letter is the direction of the diagonal line (N – downwards from left to right, Y – upwards from left to right). The bottom letter is the colour of the bigger inside shape (A – black, E – grey, Z – white).

9 A:

The first letter is the colour of the square (L – grey, O – black, Q – white). The second letter is the orientation (A – corner at the bottom, B – flat side at the bottom).

10 D:

The first letter is the colour of the medium squares (N – white, S – black, X – grey). The second letter is the colour of the small squares (C – white, F – grey, P – black).

10 Parts of nets

Page 48 Guided questions

1 D:

A, B and E are wrong because the arrow is not pointing at the circle. C is wrong because the cross should be on the opposite face.

2 B:

A, D and E are wrong because the arrow is pointing away from the single dot. C has a pattern that is not on the net.

Page 49 Guided questions

1 E:

A, B and C are wrong because the triangle is not pointing away from the circle. D has a pattern that is not on the net.

2 A:

B, C and D are wrong because the triangle is not pointing away from the black square. In E, the white circle and the triangle should be switched.

1 C:

A is wrong because the black and white squares are the wrong way around. B, D and E are wrong because the line through the circle should touch the face with the cross.

2 B:

A and C are wrong because the double arrow should point to the T shape. D and E are wrong because the base of the triangle should be by the bottom of the T shape.

1 D:

A, B and E are wrong because one of the dots should be next to the small black square. C has a pattern that is not on the net.

2 B:

A, C, D and E are wrong because the white side of the face that is half black and half white should share an edge with the face with three dots.

3 D:

A, B, and E are wrong because the two half black and half white faces are in the wrong positions. The white rectangle should share an edge with the black triangle. In C, the black triangle is not touching the face with the circle.

4 E:

A is wrong because the black triangle is not touching the spotted face. B and C are wrong because the black triangle is not touching the face with the circle. D has a pattern that is not on the net.

1 C:

A and B are wrong because the arrow is pointing away from the black square. D and E are wrong because the arrow is pointing towards the face with five dots.

2 B: A, C and E are wrong because the bottom of the smiley face should be next to one corner of the triangle. In D, the triangle is pointing at the face with dots on.

3 C: A, B and D are wrong because the face with three dots is rotated incorrectly in relation to the face with five dots. In E, the face with two dots is on the wrong side.

4 A: B, C and E are wrong because the spotted face shares an edge with a long side of the rectangle rather than with a short side. In D, the arrow is pointing to the rectangle.

5 C: A, D and E are wrong because the black square should touch the face with the striped square. B is wrong because the black square should not touch the face with the white square.

11 Which cube does the net make?

Page 52 Guided questions

1 C: A and B have patterns that are not on the net. In D, the black triangle cannot share an edge with the face with diagonal lines because it should touch the star face. In E, the face on the right should have four black dots.

2 B: A must be wrong because the double-ended arrow and the four dots should be on opposite faces. C and D must be wrong because the crossed arrows should be opposite the black square. E has a pattern that is not on the net.

Page 53 Guided questions

1 B: A and D must be wrong because the top of the T shape should be by the three dots. C must be wrong because the T shape is opposite the crossed arrows on the net, so these faces can't be next to each other. E has a pattern that is not on the net.

2 D: A and E must be wrong because the arrow should point away from the crossed black square. B and C must be wrong because the arrow should only be next to the white half of the face with black and white rectangles.

Page 53 Have a go

1 A: B must be wrong because the triangle should point away from the dot. C has a pattern that is not on the net. D and E must be wrong because the face with one black triangle should be next to the black half of the face with black and white triangles.

2 C: In A, the face with the dotted square should only touch the white half of the face with the black and white rectangles. B must be wrong because the star should be on the bottom of the cube and the face with the black and white rectangles should be on top. D must be wrong because the dotted square and the crossed square are opposite each other on the net. E has a pattern that is not on the net.

Page 54 Have a go

1 C: In A, the top face should have four dots. B has a pattern that is not on the net. In D, the side face should have a white square. E must be wrong because the face with the white square should touch the white half of the face with black and white triangles.

2 E: In A and B, the side face should be crosshatched. C and D must be wrong because the black square is opposite the crossed square on the net, so they cannot be next to each other.

3 C: In A, the front face should have black and white squares. In B, the triangle should point away from the face with black and white squares. In D, the front face should have a crosshatched circle. E must be wrong because the cross is opposite the black and white squares on the net.

4 A:

In B, the black triangle should not point left to the smiley face. In C, the front face should have a white square on a grey background. D and E must be wrong because the top of the smiley face should be next to the face with six dots.

1 A:

In B, the side face should be a crossed circle. In C, the front face should be a circle. D has a pattern that is not on the net. In E, the face with the black T shape cannot touch the face with the white square, as they should be on opposite faces of the cube.

2 E:

A must be wrong because the double-ended arrow and the white square should be on opposite faces. B must be wrong because the white triangle and the two small hexagons should be on opposite faces. In C, the triangle should point to the face with the double arrow. D has a pattern that is not on the net.

3 C:

A must be wrong because the dotted square and the thick black square should be on opposite faces. B must be wrong because the dotted square should not touch the face with the checked square. D must be wrong because the black triangle should point towards the thick black square. E must be wrong because the arrow and the checked square should be on opposite faces.

4 D:

A, B and E are wrong because the triangle should point towards the face with a black cross and away from the face with black and white rectangles. C must be wrong because the cross should be on the opposite face to the black and white rectangles.

5 A:

In B, the front face should have a black star. C must be wrong because the T shape is the wrong way around. In D, the black star is upside down. In E, the arrow should be pointing to the star.

Checkpoint 3

1 C:

A and D have faces that are not on the net. B and E are wrong because the blank faces should have shapes on them.

2 C:

A is wrong because the pentagon is rotated incorrectly. B and E are wrong because the blank faces should have patterns on them. D has a pattern that is not on the net.

3 A:

B and D are wrong because the half-white and half-black face has been rotated incorrectly. C and E are wrong because the blank face should have a shape on it.

4 E:

A and C are wrong because the triangle should point away from the crosshatched face. In B and D, the blank face should have the grey and white squares on it.

5 C:

The sides of the black triangle should be next to both the dots and the squares.

6 D:

A is wrong because the top face should have a single black line across it. In B, the circle should be opposite the square on a cross. C and E have patterns that are not on the net.

7 C:

A is wrong because the black and white squares should be next to the bottom of the smiley face. B and E have patterns that are not on the net. In D, the triangle should be opposite the black and white squares.

8 A:

B is wrong because the black square and the four hexagons should be on opposite faces. In C, the black dot and the two white dots should be on opposite faces. In D, the star and the crossed square should be on opposite faces. E has a pattern that is not on the net.

9 C:

A is wrong because the arrow should be pointing at the four dots. In B and E, the arrow should be pointing away from the circle. In D, the squares and the circle should be on opposite faces.

10 A:

B is wrong because the face with the checked square should have the circle on it. In C, the face with the circle should have the checked square on it. In D, the black stripe is rotated incorrectly. In E, the bottom of the T shape should be by the crossed square.

12 Cube views

Page 59 Guided questions

1 C:

A and B are already on the cube. D cannot be correct because you can see from the third and fourth cubes that it is opposite the blank face. E has to be opposite A.

2 D:

The first cube shows that the arrow is pointing to two patterns. D is the only answer that matches one of the patterns.

3 D:

The fourth cube shows that D is to the left of the black and white circle when the black half of the circle is on top. The first cube shows the black and white circle with the white half on top, so D must be to the right of it.

Page 59 Have a go

1 D:

A and E are already on the cube. B and C cannot be correct because the fourth cube shows that they both have to share an edge with the black square in A.

Page 60 Have a go

1 C:

The first cube shows that C is to the right of the smiley face.

2 A:

D and E are already on the cube. Comparing the third and fourth cubes shows that C is opposite the blank face. The second and third cubes show that B is opposite D.

3 B:

A and E are already on the cube. Comparing the first cube with the second cube shows that C has to be opposite the arrow face and so cannot be the blank face. D has to share an edge with the black half of A, and so cannot be the blank face.

4 A:

The first cube shows that the crossed black square is to the right of the triangle.

5 C:

A and E are already on the cube. The first cube shows that the triangle is pointing to C.

Page 61 Timed practice

1 C:

D and E are already on the cube. Comparing the first and second cubes shows that A has to be opposite the blank face. You can see from the second and third cubes that B is opposite the grey and white squares.

2 E:

The third cube shows that E has to share an edge with the black half of C.

3 B:

The second and third cubes show that the double-headed arrow has the crosshatched face above it, and the half-filled circle beneath it. In this orientation, the double-headed arrow points to the dotted square on the third cube, so the answer must be B.

4 C:

There are two faces next to the shorter sides of the crosshatched rectangle. The second cube shows that one of these faces is C, so C must be either the top or the bottom of the first cube. The second cube shows that C must be at the top of the first cube, because if it were at the bottom then the pattern with two black squares would be at the front.

5 B:

A and E are already on the cube. Comparing the first and second cubes shows you that B must be opposite D. So, B must touch the face with A on it. Three faces touch A on the first and third cubes, so the answer must be B.

13 2D views of 3D solids

Page 62 Guided questions

1 D:

The correct answer must have two squares to the left in the bottom row, two squares to the right in the middle row, and three squares in the top row.

2 E:

The correct answer must have two squares separated by a space in the bottom row, two squares to the left in the middle row, and three squares in the top row.

Page 63 Guided questions

1 D:

The correct answer must have two squares separated by a space in the bottom row, three squares in the middle row, and two squares to the left in the top row.

2 C:

The correct answer must have two squares to the right in the bottom row, two squares to the left in the middle row and two squares separated by a space in the top row.

Page 63 Have a go

1 B:

The correct answer must have two squares to the right in the bottom row, two squares to the left in the middle row and three squares in the top row.

2 B:

The correct answer must have two squares to the left in the bottom row, two squares to the right in the two middle rows and three squares in the top row.

Page 64 Have a go

1 E:

The correct answer must have two squares separated by a space in the bottom row, two squares separated by a space in the middle row, and three squares in the top row.

2 A:

The correct answer must have one square in the centre of the bottom row, two squares to the right in the middle row and two squares to the left in the top row.

3 E:

The correct answer must have one square in the centre of the bottom row, three squares in the row above, two squares to the left in the next row, and three squares in the top row.

4 D:

The correct answer must have one square to the left in the bottom row, one square to the right in the row above, two squares separated by a space in the next row and three squares in the top row.

Page 65 Timed practice

1 B:

The correct answer must have three squares in the bottom row, one square in the centre of the middle row and three squares in the top row.

2 C:

The correct answer must have one square to the left in the bottom row, two squares to the left in the middle row and two squares to the right in the top row.

3 E:

The correct answer must have one square in the centre of the bottom row, two squares to the right in the row above, one square in the centre of the next row, and three squares in the top row.

4 B:

The correct answer must have three squares in the bottom row, two squares to the right in the row above, one square to the left in the next row, and three squares in the top row.

5 E:

The correct answer must have two squares to the right in the bottom row, one square to the right in the row above, three squares in the next row, and one square to the left in the top row.

14 Fold along the line

1 B:

In A, D and E, the hexagon has been moved down, so it cannot be a reflection. In C, the hexagon has been rotated.

2 E:

In A, there is an extra diagonal line inside the hexagon. In B and D, the long diagonal line is on the wrong side. In C, the long diagonal line is missing.

Page 67 Guided questions

1 E:

In A, B and C, the triangle does not fold back on itself correctly. In D, there is an extra line.

2 C:

In A, the right-hand side has not been reflected. In B, there is only one line connecting to the bottom corner, rather than two. In D, there is no line connecting to the top corner. In E, the two lines do not meet on the reflection line.

Page 67 Have a go

1 C:

In A, none of the lines from the left-hand side are visible. In D, none of the lines from the right-hand side are visible. In B, the horizontal line is too low. In E, there are some extra lines.

2 A:

In B, the right-hand side is the wrong shape. In C, it does not fold over far enough. In D and E, it folds over too far.

Page 68 Have a go

1 B:

In A, C and E, the right-hand side has not been reflected. In D, the diagonal line inside the star is in the wrong place.

2 B:

In A, D and E, the bottom is not folded up high enough. In C, the shape in the top half of the image has moved down.

3 D: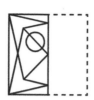

In A and B, the circle is in the wrong place. In C, some of the lines are too high up. In E, some lines are missing.

4 C:

In A, D and E, the vertical line is in the wrong place. In B, there is an extra line.

Page 69 Timed practice

1 A:

In all the other images the arrowhead is too low down.

2 E: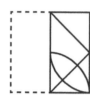

In A and B, the bottom diagonal line is the wrong way round. In C, the curved line from the left-hand side is not curved enough. In D, it is missing.

3 D:

In A, there is a line missing. In B and C, the long diagonal line does not fold up to make a symmetrical 'V'. In E, the short line from the bottom is missing.

4 D:

In A, the short diagonal line is at the wrong angle. In B, part of the circle is missing. In C, the long diagonal line is on the wrong side. In E, the bottom of the long diagonal has not been reflected.

5 C:

In A and B, one or more of the lines inside the pentagon is missing. In D, the pentagon folds up too far. In E, the pentagon does not fold up far enough.

Progress test

Page 70

1 C:

In A, the white rectangle is at the front. In B, the colours have changed. D is the same as the image on the left. In E, the shapes have moved.

2 D:

In all the other images, the spacing between the lines is wrong.

3 E:

In A, B and D, the colours of the small squares in the corners have changed. In C, the lines on the grey square in the middle are missing.

4 A:

In B, the square is too small. In C and D, the lines are at the wrong angle. In E, the square is too big.

5 E:

In A and C, the lines inside the square go from corner to corner. In B, there are no squares with a complete cross. In D, there are rectangles instead of squares.

6 D:

In A and E, the diamonds are the wrong size. In B, they are the wrong shape. In C, there are circles instead of diamonds.

7 C:

All the other images have the same number of small circles inside and outside the big circle.

8 C:

In all the other images, there are the same number of grey diamonds as white diamonds.

9 D:

The images on the left are all shapes with four sides of equal length.

10 E: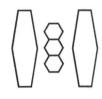

The images on the left both contain three regular shapes stacked on top of each other, with a stretched version of the shape on each side.

11 B:

A diamond shape made from the top point of the star separates. The rest of the star turns black.

12 B:

The white shapes flip vertically but stay in the same place.

13 A:

The rectangle rotates but the lines stay in the same place.

14 B: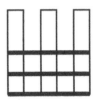

In each new image, there is one more rectangle, spaced evenly. The black lines stay in the same place, but one new line is added on top.

15 C:

The top letter is the orientation of the triangle (T – upright, P – upside down). The bottom letter is the position of the square (A – left, N – right).

16 B: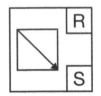

The top letter is the direction of the arrow (L – bottom left, R – bottom right, P – top right). The bottom letter is the size of the arrowhead (G – big, S – small).

17 D:

CM

The first letter is the size of the shape (R – big, V – medium, C – small). The second letter is the angle of the line (W – vertical, M – diagonal, Z – horizontal).

18 C:

OR

The first letter is the orientation of the black and white triangles (O – black upside down, A – white upside down). The second letter is the number of triangles (R – two, C – three, Z – five).

19 A:

B and C are wrong because they have faces that are not on the net. In D and E, the blank faces should have shapes on them.

Page 74

20 B:

A and C are wrong because the triangle is pointing the wrong way. In D and E, the blank faces should have shapes on them.

21 E:

A and C must be wrong, because the patterns on the front and side faces should be opposite each other. B and D have faces that are not on the net.

22 A:

B is wrong because the side face should have a checked square on it. C must be wrong because the bottom of the T shape should be next to the black and white squares. In D, the black and white squares are the wrong way around. In E, the crosshatched square and the T shape should be on opposite faces.

23 B:

It is possible to see that B is correct from the position of the dotted square on the third cube. The first cube shows that the faces next to the spotted square are A and C, so they cannot be the answer. The second and third cubes show that the faces next to the white sides are B and D. D and E are already on the cube.

24 E:

The first and fourth cubes show that the star and the two dots are on opposite faces. The blank face is next to pattern A, so the second cube tells you the correct answer must be B, C or E. The blank face can't be B, because then the side face would be E. It can't be C, because then the side face would be B. The answer must be E.

Page 75

25 A: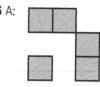

The correct answer must have two cubes to the left in the top row, one cube to the right in the middle row, and two cubes either side in the bottom row. The bottom-left cube doesn't touch any of the others.

26 A: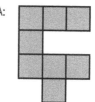

The correct answer must have three cubes in the top row, one cube to the left in the second row, three cubes in the third row, and one cube in the middle in the bottom row.

27 E:

In A, the bottom half does not fold up far enough. In B, the bottom half is a square. In C and D, the bottom folds up too far.

28 D:

In A, the lines are too close together. In B, they are too long. In C, they fold over in the wrong place. In E, the lines are at the wrong angle.

Puzzle maker

Use the templates to create your own questions.

Complete the series

Section 7

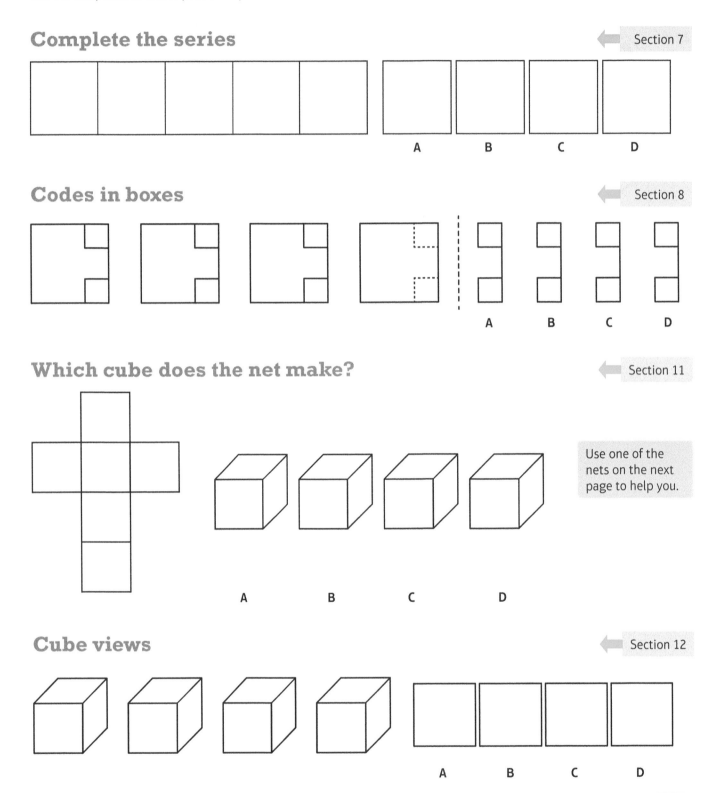

A   B   C   D

Codes in boxes

Section 8

A   B   C   D

Which cube does the net make?

Section 11

Use one of the nets on the next page to help you.

A   B   C   D

Cube views

Section 12

A   B   C   D

Cube nets

Trace the nets and cut them out. Draw patterns on them and fold them up to check your answers to the questions with cubes and nets in practice sections 10, 11 and 12.

Notes

Notes

Notes

Progress chart

Use this chart to keep track of your 11+ journey. Fill in your marks as you complete each *Timed practice* section and check off any extra practice you do.

	Timed practice	Digital questions	Ten-minute test
Diagnostic test	/28		
1 Reflection	/5	✓	✓
2 Rotation	/5	✓	✓
3 Hidden shapes	/5	✓	✓
4 Odd one out	/5	✓	✓
5 Which image belongs?	/5	✓	✓
Checkpoint 1	/10	✓	
6 Complete the pair	/5	✓	✓
7 Complete the series	/5	✓	✓
8 Codes in boxes	/5	✓	✓
9 Codes in lists	/5	✓	✓
Checkpoint 2	/10	✓	
10 Parts of nets	/5	✓	✓
11 Which cube does the net make?	/5	✓	✓
Checkpoint 3	/10	✓	
12 Cube views	/5	✓	✓
13 2D views of 3D solids	/5	✓	✓
14 Fold along the line	/5	✓	✓
Progress test	/28	✓	

Published by Pearson Education Limited, 80 Strand, London, WC2R 0RL.

www.pearsonschools.co.uk

Text and illustrations © Pearson Education Limited 2018
Edited, typeset and produced by Elektra Media Ltd
Original illustrations © Pearson Education Limited 2018
Cover illustration by Lukas Bischoff

The right of Gareth Moore to be identified as author of this work has been asserted by him in accordance with the Copyright, Designs and Patents Act 1988.

First published 2018

21 20
10 9 8 7 6 5 4 3

British Library Cataloguing in Publication Data
A catalogue record for this book is available from the British Library

ISBN: 978 1 292 24654 3

Printed by Ashford Colour Press Ltd

Note from the publisher
Pearson has robust editorial processes, including answer and fact checks, to ensure the accuracy of the content in this publication, and every effort is made to ensure this publication is free of errors. We are, however, only human, and occasionally errors do occur. Pearson is not liable for any misunderstandings that arise as a result of errors in this publication, but it is our priority to ensure that the content is accurate. If you spot an error, please do contact us at resourcescorrections@pearson.com so we can make sure it is corrected.